Blended Quilts

Blended Quilt Tips

from Marsha McCloskey's new *Blended Quilts II* book

- For your focus fabric, look for one or two large-scale spaced-floral or scenic prints with lots of colors.

- Large-scale, multicolor pictorial prints may be selectively cut for a medallion center or randomly cut for small patches.

- Pick many coordinating, go-with prints that are smaller in scale and have fewer colors than your focal prints.

- The more fabrics you use in a composition, the less they need to match.

Blended Quilts

FROM IN THE BEGINNING

MARSHA MCCLOSKEY

AND

SHARON EVANS YENTER

Dedication

To our grandchildren Katie Rose McCloskey, Jackson McCloskey,
and Zachary Danforth Yenter. Our quilts are our link with the past but
you are our connection to the future. May you help create a world of tolerance,
hope, and understanding. A big expectation for such little people!
Learn, create, pray, love, and visit Grandma often.

Foreword

Sharon Yenter and Marsha McCloskey met over 25 years ago in the early days of the current quiltmaking renaissance. The first major museum exhibition of quilts was at the Whitney Museum of American Art in New York City in 1971. It was an unprecedented event and validated mostly "women's work" as art worthy of being displayed in a prestigious setting. Anonymous may have been a woman but her talents were coming to the forefront.

The bicentennial celebration of 1976 stimulated the nation's interest in history and, as women wanted to explore links to their past and express pride in their country, the art was rediscovered and a quiltmaking revival was born.

At that time, Marsha and Sharon were raising young children. They both felt the need for a creative outlet and additional cash for the family budget. A fascination with antique quilts and an admiration for the detail of traditional patchwork patterns led them to create their own products and offer them for sale at street fairs and craft shows. They took the postal mantra to heart, so neither snow, nor rain, nor heat, nor gloom of night kept them from their appointed booths!

After Marsha had constructed over 2000 potholders and Sharon had stitched over 400 machine appliquéd wallhangings, they decided it was time to give up production sewing. They had paid their dues. So much for the glamour and excitement of the streets! Their home lives consisted of sweet children admiring Mom's 3rd or 13th effort of the day, a husband good-naturedly grumbling "where's dinner?" and growing collections of boring 1970s fabrics which were lovingly stockpiled.

They abandoned their booths, but they weren't about to abandon their newfound creativity. There were converts to be made. The quilt world needed them and they were going to spread the word.

Marsha opted for teaching and writing books, and Sharon chose to open a quilt shop in Seattle...with Marsha as her first teacher. Both women realized the importance of creativity in their own lives and felt the need to give positive feedback to others.

Never again would a woman finish a creative project, only to find that there was no one to admire it. With Sharon's store and Marsha's classes there came a built-in appreciative audience in the form of staff members, like-minded customers, and excited students. Knowledge, enthusiasm, and praise flowed, and continues to flow.

In the years since their meeting, Marsha has written 20 books, made hundreds of quilts, and introduced thousands of students to the history and joys of quiltmaking.

Sharon has written three books, ordered tons of fabric, only dreamed of making hundreds of quilts, and welcomed thousands of guests and students to her colorful and trend-setting quilt shop, In The Beginning Fabrics, now in its 25th year of business.

Introduction

In the late 1980s, Sharon expanded her store and added decorating fabrics to the inventory. The beautiful chintz fabrics were intoxicating and reminiscent of a long-ago era. The designs included large and medium florals, toiles, and stripes, and each floral was printed in multiple screens of up to 20 different colors. By contrast, most of the fabrics available for quilting at that time contained only two to six screens, resulting in printed designs that were simple and uncomplicated and contributed to quilts that contained few colors carefully coordinated.

About that time, Marsha had the opportunity to teach in South Carolina. Her hostesses showed her the sights, including the Charleston Museum in Charleston, S.C.

In the museum she discovered an extensive collection of vibrant chintz quilts and captivating pieces from the early 19th century.

Marsha's quiltmaking at that time featured intricate piecing, muted color tones, and small prints, and many of her quilts borrowed from traditional pieced designs popular in the late 1800s. The museum visit and the availability of large chintz florals gave her the impetus to follow an old/new way of quiltmaking by resurrecting concepts developed in the early days of our country.

Sharon and Marsha started working with the chintz floral fabrics, making new quilts with the feeling of quilts from the early 1800s. They offered a class at In The Beginning in which students were encouraged to use large-scale chintz florals in easy, uncomplicated, pieced designs. The students were always excited with their quilts but the rest of the quilt world was concerned about hand quilting through the heavy chintz (machine quilting had not yet gained widespread acceptance), and shop owners were leery about having large decorator floral bolts in their stores.

Sharon and Marsha decided the quilt world wasn't ready for their concept. Marsha returned to her traditional small-scale piecing and Sharon continued to tend her quilt shop. Several years went by before Sharon visited Great Britain, studied the glorious quilts residing there, and was lucky enough to purchase an early English chintz quilt.

Marsha's interest in large-scale prints continued to grow when she went on a teaching trip to the Netherlands. It was there that she discovered an exciting quilt history of Dutch quiltmakers using large-scale florals and simple patterns.

Through their separate experiences, Marsha and Sharon's commitment to their concept was revived. In the mid-90s, Sharon had the opportunity to design fabric. Her first effort was a group that included elegant large florals reminiscent of the early chintzes. Sharon and Marsha continue to design fabrics with these elements, and many other fabric manufacturers currently offer lovely reproductions which are appropriate also. Now quilters can hand quilt through these designs and replicate the quilts of the early 1800s. Perhaps the Quilt World is now ready!

This Ohio Star quilt was made in Pennsylvania in the 1830s.
It features a luxurious chintz, possibly purchased for the quilt,
and a beautiful collection of small prints, plaids, and stripes.
Collection of In The Beginning Fabrics, Seattle, WA.

Table of Contents

History

The history of quiltmaking in America owes its foundation to the many immigrants who brought their knowledge and work habits with them to their new country. The Colonies of the late 1700s were populated with people who spun flax into linen and wove wool into cloth for the necessities of everyday life. Much of the spinning and weaving was done by the children of the family to help their already over-burdened mother who had to contend with growing and preserving food, cooking, sewing, cleaning, and never-ending pregnancies.

Before the Revolutionary War in 1775, few but the well-to-do could afford the luxurious imported chintzes and cottons that arrived aboard clipper ships at the ports of Baltimore, Charleston, Philadelphia, and New York. For the common person, printed fabric was in short supply so each piece was a tiny treasure. England allowed no printing machines to be sent to America and banned any emigration by printers.

Prior to the War of Independence, the Colonies supplied to England many raw materials including cotton. The cotton was woven and printed in England and returned as expensive fabric which was heavily taxed. In 1765, England passed the Stamp Act which increased taxes even more and made the Colonists determined to spin and weave their own linen and wool and boycott British goods entirely.

Observing the habit of saving and trading precious printed cotton fabrics for a special quilt, one writer, in the book, *Artists in Aprons: Folk Art by American Women*, noted that "a woman made ragged utility quilts as fast as she could so her family wouldn't freeze, and she made one as beautiful as she could so her heart wouldn't break."

Ninepatch Chain, *made by a bride of English descent in Chester County, Pennsylvania, circa 1832. Notice the diagonal flow across the quilt and the English copperplate chintz. 102" x 102".*
Reproduced by permission of the American Museum in Britain, Bath ©.

Dutch Coverlet, *circa 1830. A multitude of exuberant fabrics in chintz and cottons of varying sizes illuminate this coverlet. Notice the central motif of the woman on the elephant. 56" x 69½".*
Photograph: Nederlands Openluchtmuseum, Arnhem, The Netherlands.

The custom of making one time-consuming handsome quilt for special occasions seems to have permitted the survival of a relatively large number of glorious quilts spanning the years 1780-1840. Utility quilts from that era no longer exist, but excellent examples of quilts containing printed fabrics survive in museum holdings and private collections.

After eight years of war, Britain recognized the independence of her colonies by signing the Peace Treaty of 1783. The new American citizens were free to weave and print their own textiles. Imports continued to pour in from France, England, and the Netherlands, for the new United States had a non-native population of some seven million inhabitants and was an important trading partner.

In the early 1800s, Britain resumed its long struggle with France and the armies of Napoleon. In 1807, an American warship in U.S. waters, the U.S.S. Chesapeake, was inexplicably fired upon by a British frigate. The U.S. cut off all trade with France and Britain with the Embargo Act of 1807. Unrest continued to escalate and on June 17, 1812, Congress voted for war and the second War of Independence began. Trade had been disrupted for many years and European fabric was becoming scarce. The word

Top: **English-Style Frame Quilt,** *circa 1820-1830, made in Fauquier County, Virginia, by Rebecca Ellen (Davenport) Blackwell. Block printed linens and cottons. 105½" x 106".*
Collection of the Daughters of the American Revolution Museum, Washington, DC. Gift of Lucy S.B. Jones.

Bottom: **Dutch Patchwork Quilt,** *circa 1800-1825. Made from triangles of chintz and printed cotton. Shades of light and dark are pieced in a seemingly random fashion but make an interesting abstract design. 80½" x 106".*
Photograph: Nederlands Openluchtmuseum, Arnhem, The Netherlands.

"chintzy," meaning cheap, was coined reportedly because every scrap of chintz fabric was saved in a miserly fashion, rather than shared with friends as were most cottons.

The last war fought on American soil with a foreign nation was finally resolved with the Peace Treaty of 1815. Europe realized that the United States was a strong unified nation.

Peace reigned at last and there was an absolute explosion of fabric choice at home and abroad. By 1825, millions of yards of printed fabrics were being produced. The roller printing machine was perfected for general usage in the U.S. and business was booming. French author and historian Alexis de Tocqueville wrote in the 1830s after having observed the U.S.: "If anyone asks me what I think is the chief cause of the extraordinary prosperity and growing power of this nation, I should answer that it is due to the superiority of their women."

After years of war, struggles, and uncertainty, American women were ready to create art and beauty to bring aesthetic and spiritual sustenance to their lives.

The largest influences in American quilt-making came from the Dutch and English communities combined with textile design and color from France and India. By the beginning of the 19th century, the city of New York had sixty thousand inhabitants. Many of these were Dutch and their quilt-making skills blossomed. Unlike American and British quilts, those from the Netherlands cannot be categorized by a consistent pattern. Most are composed of a series of shapes; usually squares, triangles, and strips. The fabrics are bold in design and color, building a collage of exquisite textiles.

The majority of British colonial quilts would be described as Frame Quilts. Many featured a central panel, framed by a series of borders skill-fully pieced together from many differently-sized prints. If the quilts contain pieced patterns, it is usually a simple star, ninepatch, windmill, or triangles set together. The profusion of pieced

This strippy quilt was discovered at a flea market in the outskirts of Paris. The quilt dates from around 1900, but many of the French textiles are copies of an earlier period. It was apparently made from swatch books; you can see three places where the labels were torn off, and many of the fabrics repeat in multiple colorways. The back is made of sugar sacks from Colorado, USA. Note the "Extra Fine" wording where the backing fabric is brought to the front. 63" x 74".
Collection of In The Beginning Fabrics, Seattle, WA.

designs with American names came in the later part of the 19th century. Wide floral borders became common as pioneer women had access to more fabric choice and family beds became larger. An elegant panel of chintz represented prosperity and was often incorporated into a "best quilt." With a shortage of bedrooms, many colonial parlors contained a large bed that, when company was present, was covered with a "best quilt" made of an abundance of colorful fabrics for guests to admire. "Best quilts" were carefully stored away and many survive today because they were rarely used for more than occasional display.

Blended Quilts

We decided on the name Blended Quilts because it is appropriate on several levels. It includes a blending of our quiltmaking styles, ideas, and experiences, and we realized that the definitions found in the dictionary are very appropriate to this technique.

blended: (blend-ed)

1. to combine so as to make parts indistinguishable

2. to mix thoroughly so as to obtain a new mixture

3. to merge or become merged into one: unite

With this technique we blend large, medium, and small prints together to create a pleasing and harmonious whole. The most important consideration with the blended technique is to allow fabric designs to flow into each other, colors to mix and merge to create a new composition, and geometric shapes to blend for unusual and eclectic combinations.

The early American women used their special pieces of fabric in seemingly random placings, yet bold and original quilts were made. The size and scale of certain prints forced women to work in the abstract, or perhaps they chose to be liberated artistically and created dynamic compositions purposely and with confidence.

When the two of us first started making blended quilts we realized that we were breaking many of the traditional rules we had learned about quiltmaking. The necessity of contrast was unimportant, the habit of using only small prints was wrong, and regular geometric patterns were not relevant to this technique.

It was a "freeing" experience when we realized that these quilts had very different rules than we were used to. In fact, they had very few design and color regulations.

For the blended technique, we recommend that you forget many things you have learned and look at quiltmaking in a fresh way. The quilts featured are influenced by the unique quilts of the late 1700s and early 1800s and have little resemblance to later quilts. It will be difficult to break the rules at first, but if you take the leap it will be fun and liberating. Let yourself go!

Take a journey back to 1800. Imagine that you have no access to quilt shops or any convenient source of fabric. Most of the available fabric is imported from England or France. You have precious chintz scraps from your draperies, leftover cotton fragments of dresses, bits procured by trading with friends, and several colorways of the same print purchased from a traveling peddler. You own a limited selection of light, medium, and dark fabrics.

You have very few decisions about color because few colors are available. Your skills to create a painterly masterpiece must be developed by blending the colors you own, rotating floral patterns, and choosing appropriate and pleasing combinations from the scant fabrics in your collection. You must work with what you have and make the most of your precious supply.

In spite of these limitations, you can create elegant and spectacular quilts.

The quilts in this book have plenty of large spaces to showcase colorful, large-scale florals or scenics much as quilters did with their prized quilts in the early part of the 19th century.

In our quilts we keep the piecing simple and let the fabric do the work. Before you start the projects in this book, it is important that you read through the book to recognize the important elements of the blended technique. Turn to the *Basic Quiltmaking Techniques* on page 24. Many basic instructions not fully covered in the individual project directions are presented there.

We have identified sixteen elements that are important to achieve the look you want in your blended quilts. Each quilt in the book features several elements but only one will be emphasized with each project. You may want to read each pattern preface and study each quilt to get a complete understanding of our methods.

When you're ready to begin, we recommend that you plan your quilt on a design wall. Audition fabric and cut patches as you go. Select your focal fabric or fabrics first, then choose many other prints that relate in color and style. It is nearly impossible to see elements of design and color interplay on a horizontal surface. A painter very rarely works on the floor or a table-top with good reason. A vertical surface allows design elements to appear and color and contrast to be immediately visible and open to change. As you add pieces to your design wall, let the print in one patch blend visually with the next. Intentionally "lose" the design, then find it again. Stand back often to get an overall view.

Be bold, vary the contrast in different areas of the design. Blend the printed designs in one area into the next by using similar prints and values next to each other. Shape and direct what the viewer sees by creating a few areas of higher con-trast. Use darker, brighter, or lighter accent colors to add spice and interest. The design wall allows you to experiment with the placement of each piece, until each one is placed to your satisfaction.

Marsha gets advice and assistance from her granddaughter, Katie Rose, at the design wall. Notice their blended clothing.

For your design wall you may use needle-punch, flannel, thin quilt batting, muslin, or a product called "Quilt Wall®." Your design wall should be large enough to accommodate your quilt pieces. In figuring design wall dimensions, allow approximately 16" surrounding your planned top to allow for the total seam allowances of your quilt. Sew design wall materi-als together if you need additional width.

Most flannel, needlepunch, and muslin is 44" wide. Batting width varies, and Quilt Wall® is 72" x 72".

Supplies

In addition to the materials listed for each quilt, you will need the following basic sewing supplies:

- Rotary cutting mat, rulers, and cutter
- Precision Trimmer 3™ *(a ruler designed by Marsha McCloskey and featured in this book)*
- Scissors: 1 for plastic, 1 for fabric
- Design wall
- Pins
- Steam iron
- Sewing machine
- Thread

Fabric Choices

All blended quilts are scrap quilts, although they contain very selective, unique pieces of cloth that would never have been referred to as scraps by our ancestors. The early quilts (1790-1840) contained many expensive pieces of elegant fabric. These were not the patched quilts of the westward pioneers where you might find a two-inch square composed of three splinters of cloth.

The blended quilts were "best quilts". Large and medium florals were used to create sophisticated arrangements in colors that were sometimes bright and were, at other times, colonial shades of celadon, mulberry, cornflower, and buttery yellow. Bouquets of glorious flowers blended with vines and birds to create imaginative compositions.

Toile de Jouy/Scenics

Chintz

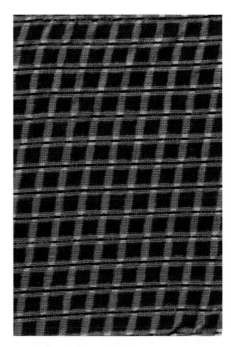

Plaids

Let's examine the fabrics necessary for a successful blended quilt.

Reproduction fabrics from the early to late 1800s are important to create the rich, vintage grandeur of the early quilts. All quilt shops have collections of these fabrics. You may have to purchase from several manufacturers but that will add to the interest of your quilt. Large floral bouquet fabrics and scenics do not have to be exact reproductions; in fact, a more clear contemporary look is sometimes preferable.

FABRIC STYLES
Toile de Jouy

Pronounced twahl duh zhwee, the name means "fabric of Jouy." This cloth was originally produced by copperplate printing at the Oberkampf factory in Jouy, France. Historic scenes, as well as romanticized scenic motifs, were traditionally portrayed. Since its beginning in 1770, toile has been considered the most popular fabric of France.

Scenics

Large, multi-color scenic designs with forest, animal, or garden motifs work well combined with florals or small prints.

Chintz or "chintz like"

Chintz is a polished cotton usually containing large or medium florals in rich, elegant colorways. This fabric originated in India in the 17th century. Floral bouquet motifs suitable for blended quilts may be made of chintz or light-weight cottons.

Plaids

Plaids in coordinating colors are very appropriate combined with florals or small prints.

Stripes

Shirting stripes in neutral colors are workable as blenders. Intricate patterns of stripes and flowers similar to those produced in France in the 1700s are wonderful for borders, or they may be cut selectively for piecing.

Stripes

Small Prints

Picotage

Small Prints

Small "viney" or flowing prints work well with the blending technique. Many hues and shades of beige and neutrals are necessary to fill in spaces so more colorful pieces can be starred. Small-scale cotton prints were very popular in the early 19th century as they were used in clothing for the working classes. Many of the designs consisted of floral "sprig" motifs on a pastel ground. Roses were popular and were included in many minia-ture designs. The use of tone-on-tone florals, eclectic elements, trailing ribbons, cherubs, urns, and picotage were common.

Picotage

In France, Christophe-Phillipe Oberkampf introduced the picotage effect by using metal pins to make small dots on the fabric surface. He interspersed these among florals and tonal patterns to create a shaded design. Look for various beige tones and soft grayed pastels with flowers and picotage in the many reproduction fabrics available today.

Paisleys

The curvy, intricate scrollwork designs that we have come to know as Paisley were originated in India during the 1600s, but did not arrive in France until the early 1800s.

Manufacturers block printed these designs for garments and home furnishings, and Paisley-style designs became an important fabric motif throughout the 1800s. These patterns work especially well in quilts as they lend a soft, graceful, multi-colored look.

Medium Floral Prints

Spaced florals that can flow into a larger bou-quet are necessary to maintain the lines of color. The tightly packed florals used in the watercolor quilt technique do not work here. There must be space and background around the floral motifs to allow the patterns to merge one into another.

Miscellaneous Fabrics

These are those special pieces you've been collecting for a unique project. An elegant jacquard, a Japanese kimono swatch, a vintage pet print, a remnant from an eventful trip. You can incorporate any of these into your design plan.

Paisleys

Medium Floral Prints

Miscellaneous Fabrics

Always be on the lookout for interesting pieces. Take your Precision Trimmer 3™ ruler to the store with you and use it as a viewer to discover interesting bits of fabric. Sometimes a piece you ordinarily would never consider purchasing has a color or element that might be the perfect addition to your project.

Geometrics

Geometrics have been around for a long time and many 19th century prints are charmingly abstract. These designs are a favored choice to please men when too many florals appear on a quilt top. Geometrics can be curvy circles, stars, triangles, or squares, plus many more choices and combinations. They mix beautifully with florals and are an inspired addition to blended quilts.

Coral/Seaweed

Coral, serpentine, and seaweed prints were popular in the early- to mid-1800s. They feature undulating designs reminiscent of objects seen at the seashore. Their organic curves blend beautifully and will bring any quilt out of the doldrums. Use small, randomly cut pieces to add a special zing to your quilts.

Tone-on-tone

Tone-on-tone prints are monochromatic designs which can sometimes be used as "textured solids." They are much more interesting than solids but do not interrupt the flow of your design. You may want to use them to add a bright "zinger" color, or a light or dark color. Keep a grouping of these fabrics in your stash and you will be able to put blocks together easily. Blended quilts use many beige or neutral shades of fabric so be aware of interesting pieces on your shopping expeditions.

Geometrics

Coral/Seaweed

Tone-on-tone

Color and Design

A Starting Point: Choose a large floral bouquet or a scenic design, or both, which contain many screens of color. This will be your focus fabric. Identify the colors in the print by matching them to fabrics in your collection. You will often find color screen markings on the fabric selvage. If you have these, your job will be easier. The dots tell you the number of colors in your print.

The print shown, at right, has twelve screens, which will give you a wonderful selection of color. When picking companion prints to go with your focus fabric, keep in mind that pieces you choose from your stash may have more than one color in them. Try to choose companion prints containing no more than three or four colors.

Lay your fabrics out on a table or put pieces on a design wall. Refer to your chosen quilt pattern. Determine where you would like your focus fabric to be, and the proportions of your color placement.

Pin your focus fabric to a design wall. Try auditioning toiles, plaids, stripes, beige to gold small prints, some darks, a large floral, or tone-on-tone designs for your project. You may want to cut small sample swatches. Four or seven inch squares are good sizes, because they may be reused in your quilt or another project. The only mistake you might make with this technique is to use too much of one kind of fabric. A large number of packed florals, for instance, might make a lovely watercolor quilt, but it creates a disastrous blended quilt. This is a scrap quilt, and areas where your eyes can rest are important to accent the design of your project.

Consider some bright greens, sparkly reds, and cheddar yellows for areas of intense color. Work with as many colors as you want. Pin pieces on your design wall and stand back and critique. You may have three to ten pieces of beige, including greenish, taupe, and warm; or greens in acid, lime, celadon, forest, and more. These colors are not meant to match. Stretch yourself! A quilt that is too "matchy" can be a boring quilt and not true

"This designing on the wall with Grandma is too much fun!" says Katie Rose.

Fabric courtesy of Marcus Brothers Textiles: French Connection Collection, a group of 1800s reproduction fabrics designed by Judie Rothermel.

to the period. Our ancestors did not have coordinating fabric groups. You want people to spend time looking at your design and fabric. Blended quilts ask for attention. That is what makes them wonderful wall quilts. A cursory glance will not do. Their quirky compositions demand study.

TRANSITIONS

Forget much of what you have learned about low contrast being a mistake in quiltmaking. Many prints of similar value fabric in blended quilts will be allowed to flow into others, creating a gentle transition. Splashes of color relate one fabric to another by color or pattern and disguise the seam lines. Your low-contrast prints should blend into each other and create a rich tapestry of warmth.

Transition #1 features a large floral print with a red background. We have picked red motifs in a toile, flowing floral, and sprigged design to shift the background color from red to beige. Notice how the size of the motifs becomes smaller and makes your eyes read the whole transition.

Transition #2 illustrates a large floral in soft pink tones with a light background. We have picked up the color in the large flowers to flow through the transition. The motifs change size but the color remains pink. Notice the flowers from the first two fabrics blending together to continue the bouquet. It is important to stand back from your project as you're working on blending florals. Practice with larger pieces of fabric and cut only when you're happy with the flow.

Transition #3 shows three florals blending together by color; from realistic flowers to a stylized floral motif. Notice how the pink background changes to beige. The light beige opens up the option of continuing with a traditional high-contrast block, or staying light and creating a restful area which is sometimes necessary in your quilt.

Transition #4—Many quilts from the 1800s contained three or four of the same fabric in different colorways. These fabrics can be blended by pattern to make a continuous flow that continues the design, but changes the background color. This technique works well in borders or large squares.

1. Fold one of the fabrics on the crosswise grain and press firmly.
2. Place on top of other fabric and adjust until design matches.
3. Unfold top fabric and pin on press line.
4. Make sure pattern matches and stitch. Cut to size after sewing.

Contrast

We've highlighted a traditional block that features high contrast. This could be used with Transition #3 to create a more vibrant quilt. Your eyes stop and take notice of the abrupt design and color change. We've picked up hues from the transition in darker shades for a pleasing contrast.

Basic Quiltmaking Techniques

MAKING YOUR QUILT TOP

Rotary Cutting Basics

Our goal with the patterns in *Blended Quilts* is to make the cutting and stitching simple and easy, so you can concentrate on the fun of blending fabric colors and prints. For these quilts, you will only need to cut three basic shapes: squares, rectangles, and triangles. Even the more complex shapes like those in the setting squares on Sharon's Fourpatch Strippy on page 82 are made with "flip and sew" methods that involve only squares.

The basic tools for cutting fabric patches are a rotary cutter, ruler, and mat. If you don't already own rotary cutting tools, choose a cutter that fits comfortably in your hand, a self-healing mat, and an acrylic ruler that measures at least 6" x 18" and is marked with measurements in ¼" and ⅛" increments.

If you have never done rotary cutting, practice on scrap fabric first. The blade is very sharp; it is not necessary to press very hard when you first begin, but be sure to place even pressure on the blade as you cut. Always remember to: keep your fingers and other body parts away from the blade, close the blade each time you finish cutting, and keep the cutter out of the reach of children. The cutter can be dangerous if not used with proper care.

Cutting Strips From Yardage

In quilts, long strips of fabric are used for borders, and shorter ones are used for lattices. Narrow strips are used in some design blocks. The rotary method of cutting squares and rectangles begins with cutting strips of fabric. So you will be cutting lots of strips. Strips can be cut on the lengthwise grain (parallel to the selvage) or crosswise grain (perpendicular to the selvage). All strips are cut with the ¼-inch seam allowance included.

To cut strips with crosswise grain, fold the fabric selvage to selvage, aligning the cross and straight grains as best you can. Place fabric on the rotary cutting mat with the folded edge closest to your body. Make the first cut to trim away the uneven raw edges of fabric, creating a straight edge that is perpendicular to the fold. Align a square plastic cutting ruler with the fold of the fabric and place a cutting ruler to the left.

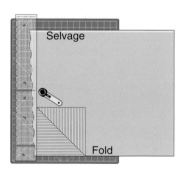

Clare of Assisi

When making all cuts, fabric should be placed to your right. (If you are left handed, reverse the directions.) Remove the square plastic cutting ruler and make a rotary cut along the right side of the ruler. While holding the ruler firmly in place, position the blade of the cutter alongside the ruler at the end closest to you. Cutting through all layers, roll the cutter away from you.

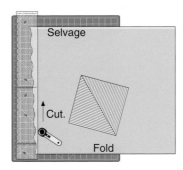

To keep the ruler from slipping while cutting, pause occasionally and move your hand up on the ruler to maintain even pressure. Make successive cuts measuring from the first cut as shown.

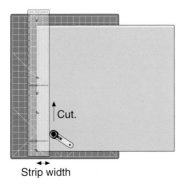

To cut strips on lengthwise grain, fold and position the fabric so cuts will be parallel to the selvage. Make the first cut parallel to the selvage close enough to trim it away and create a clean edge from which to measure. Make successive cuts measuring from the first cut.

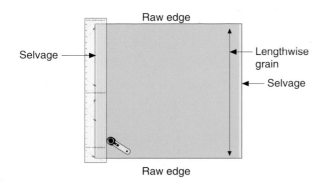

Cutting Strips From Fat Quarters

A fat quarter yard is a piece of fabric that measures 18" x 21". Quilters like fat quarters because they provide more useable fabric than quarter yards measured off the bolt at 9". Quilt stores often sell precut fat quarters one at a time or in coordinated packets. It's a great way to get a wide variety of prints for your collection for not a lot of money.

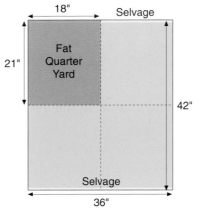

Divide a yard of fabric (36" x 42") in half the long way; then divide the resulting section in half to make 4 "fat" quarter yards, each measuring 18" x 21".

Many of our patterns call for cutting strips from fat quarters. If the pattern calls for 17"-18" strips, you can cut the strips across the short dimension, parallel to the selvage.

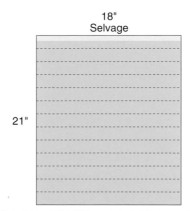

Cut strips 17"-18" long parallel to the selvage.

If the pattern calls for 20+" strips, cut the strips the long dimension, perpendicular to the selvage.

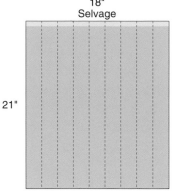

Cut strips 20+" long perpendicular to the selvage.

Squares and Rectangles

First cut fabric in strips the measurement of the finished square plus seam allowances. Using the square plastic cutting ruler, align the top and bottom edge of strip and cut fabric into squares the same width as the strip.

Cut rectangles in the same manner, first cutting strips the width of the finished rectangle plus seam allowances, then cutting to the proper length.

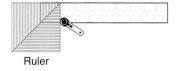

Ruler

Triangles

Cut fabric in strips, then into squares the size specified in the instructions. The measurements given for half- and quarter-square triangles in the quilt directions include ¼" seam allowances.

Half-Square Triangles

If you need a triangle with the straight grain on the short side, cut half-square triangles. Cut a square, then cut it in half diagonally once. The resulting two triangles will have short sides on the straight grain of the fabric and the long side on the bias.

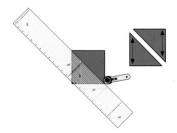

Quarter-Square Triangles

If you need a triangle with the straight grain on the long side, cut quarter-square triangles. Cut a square, then cut it in half diagonally twice. The resulting four triangles will have the long side on the straight grain and the short sides on the bias.

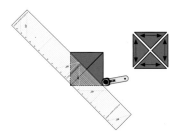

Machine Piecing

To make a pieced design block, sew the smallest pieces together first to form units. Join smaller units to form larger ones until the block is complete. Diagrams with each quilt pattern show the order in which to sew the patches together.

Use 100 percent cotton thread as light as the lightest fabric in the project. Most quilters choose one color of thread—usually white or a neutral color—and use it to piece the whole quilt regardless of color changes in the fabric.

Sew exact ¼" seams. On some machines the width of the presser foot is ¼" and can be used as a guide. If you don't have such a foot, you'll need to establish the proper seam allowance on your sewing machine. Place a piece of quarter- or eighth-inch graph paper under the presser foot and gently lower the needle onto the line that is ¼" from the edge of the paper. Lay a piece of masking tape at the edge of the paper to act as the ¼" guide.

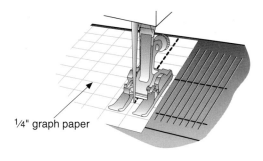

¼" graph paper

For the patterns in this book, sew from cut edge to cut edge. Backtack if you wish, but when a seam line will be crossed and held by another, it is not necessary. Clip threads as you go. Make it a habit. Threads left hanging from the ends of seam lines can get in the way and be a real nuisance.

Use chain piecing whenever possible to save time and thread. To chain piece, sew one seam, but do not lift the presser foot. Do not take the piece out of the sewing machine and do not cut the thread. Instead, set up the next seam to be sewn and stitch as you did the first. There will be a little twist of thread between the two pieces. Sew all the seams you can at one time in this way, then remove the "chain." Clip the threads.

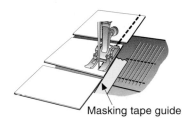

Masking tape guide

Pinning

Pin seams before stitching if matching is involved, if your seams are longer than 4", or if your fabrics are a little slippery. Pin points of matching (where seam lines or points meet) first. Once these important points are firmly in place, pin the rest of the seam, easing if necessary (see Easing on page 28). Keep pins away from seam lines, as sewing over them tends to damage the needle and makes it hard to be accurate in tight places.

Pressing

In this book, most seams are pressed to one side, toward the darker fabric whenever possible. Sometimes, for matching purposes, seams are pressed in opposite directions, regardless of which is the darker fabric. We sometimes press seams open to distribute bulk, as in the Pinwheel design on page 92.

Press with a dry iron that has a shot of steam when needed. Take care not to overpress. First, press the sewn seam flat to "set" it. Next, press the seam open or to the side as desired. Press from both the right and wrong sides to make the seam flat without little pleats at the ends.

Matching

1. Opposing seams. When stitching one seamed unit to another, press seam allowances on seams that need to match in opposite directions. The two "opposing" seams will hold each other in place and evenly distribute the bulk.

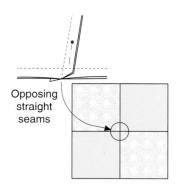

Opposing straight seams

Often, the opposing seams are diagonal seams. Plan pressing to take advantage of opposing seams.

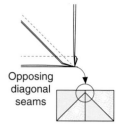

Opposing diagonal seams

2. Positioning pin. Carefully push a pin straight through two points that need to match. Pull the pin tight to establish the proper point of matching. Pin the seam normally and remove the positioning pin before stitching.

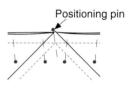

Positioning pin

3. The **X**. When triangles are pieced, stitches will form an **X** at the next seam line. Stitch through the center of the **X** to make sure the points on the sewn triangles will not be chopped off.

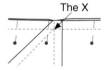

The X

4. Easing. When two pieces to be sewn together are supposed to match but instead are slightly different lengths, pin the points of matching and lightly steam press the seam before stitching. Stitch with the shorter piece on top. The feed dog eases the fullness of the bottom piece.

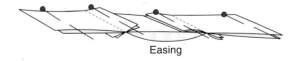

Easing

Check Your Work

Piecing a quilt top is always easier if you are accurate and check your work as you go along. Many of our quilts use pieced units (half- and quarter-square triangle units and fourpatches) that finish at 3". This means that before these units are sewn to other pieces, they should measure exactly 3½" from raw edge to raw edge.

Use Marsha McCloskey's Precision Trimmer 3™ to check your work. Position the ruler on the pieced units as pictured and trim the edges to make perfect 3½" squares.

Trim to 3½".

Setting the Quilt Blocks Together

When design blocks and setting pieces (large squares, triangles, and/or lattice strips) are sewn together to make a quilt top, it is called the "set." Each quilt pattern has a Quilt Assembly Diagram showing how the parts will be sewn together in rows. Sometimes the rows go across the quilt and sometimes on the diagonal. When sewing the rows together, press for opposing seams and pin all points of matching.

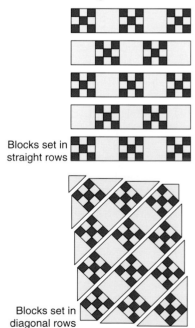

Blocks set in straight rows

Blocks set in diagonal rows

Borders

The borders for most of the quilts in this book are wide strips of fabric sewn to the sides and then to the top and bottom edges of the quilt top. If you prefer mitered corners for any of the quilts that have straight-sewn corners, you may need additional yardage to cut longer border strips.

1. To cut the two side borders to the right length, measure the quilt top length (including seam allowances) through the center. (On large quilts, it's a good idea to measure the length along both outer edges as well and use an average of the three measurements.) Cut the two strips this length.
2. Mark the center and quarter points on both the quilt top and border strips.
3. Matching ends, centers, and quarter points, pin border strips to the quilt top. Pin generously and press along the matched edges to set the seam before sewing. A shot of steam will help with any easing that might be required.
4. Using a ¼" seam allowance, stitch the border to the quilt top. Press the seam allowance to one side as directed in the quilt instructions.
5. Repeat steps 1-4 to measure the quilt width, including the borders just added, cut, and attach the top and bottom borders.

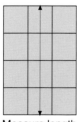
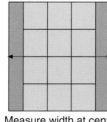
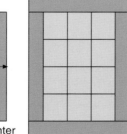

Measure length at center.   Measure width at center after adding side borders.

FINISHING YOUR QUILT

Plan and Mark Quilting Designs

The fabrics used in *Blended Quilts* make a quilt surface rich and complex in design and color. Frankly, too many fancy quilting designs on these quilts would be a waste of effort because you couldn't see them. All of our quilts were quilted by machine. We tried to plan simple designs to complement our simple piecing.

Quilting lines should be evenly distributed over the quilt surface. Directions that come with your batting will tell how close the quilting lines must be to keep the batting from coming apart when the quilt is washed. Avoid tight complicated designs that then require similar quilting over the whole quilt. Likewise avoid leaving large areas unquilted.

Some quilters prefer to mark their quilt top with quilting lines before it is assembled with the backing and batting. To do this, you will need marking pencils; a long ruler or yardstick; stencils or templates for quilting motifs; and a smooth, clean, hard surface on which to work. Thoroughly press the quilt top. Use a sharp marking pencil and lightly mark the quilting lines on the fabric. No matter what kind of marking tool you use, light lines will be easier to remove than heavy ones.

Backing and Batting

Prepare the backing. For quilts that measure more than 38" wide, you will need to make the backing by cutting and sewing two or more lengths of fabric together.

1. Add 8" to the length and width of the completed quilt top for a working allowance (4" all the way around).
2. To make a backing that is large enough, cut lengths of fabric and sew them together on the long sides. Press the seams open. You can sew two lengths together with one center seam, or split the second length and sew the pieces to each side of the other length of

fabric. Sometimes, to save fabric, it is best to cut and piece the backing so the seam runs across the width of the quilt.

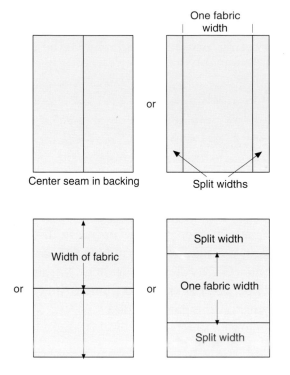

3. Choose a thin, cotton or cotton-polyester blend batting in a size that is longer and wider than your quilt top. Trim batting to size of backing.

Layering the Quilt

1. Lay the backing face down on a large, clean, flat surface—the floor or a large table. With masking tape, tape the backing down to keep it smooth and flat while you are working with the other layers. If you are working on a table, part of the quilt will probably hang over the sides. Begin in the quilt center and work in sections toward the sides and ends.

2. Gently lay the batting on top of the backing, centering and smoothing it as you go.

3. Center the freshly ironed quilt top on top of the batting, right side up. Starting in the middle, gently smooth out fullness to the sides and corners. Take care not to distort the straight lines of the quilt design and the borders.

4. Baste the layers together with safety pins or needle and light-colored thread. Start in the middle and make a line of long stitches to each corner to form a large **X**. Continue basting in a grid of parallel lines 6"-8" apart. Finish with a row of basting around the outside edges—¼" away from the edge.

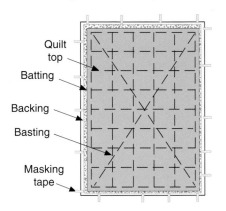

Quilting

Quilt the layers together by hand or machine. This is a little sentence to cover a big subject. There are whole books written on how to quilt. There are also many machine quilting services that will do the quilting for you. Here are a few things to consider before you decide on your quilting method: First, how are you going to use the quilt? Will it be a rarely-used heirloom quilt, or do you plan to use the quilt daily? Heirloom quilts are often enhanced by hand-quilting. Everyday quilts may be better served by quick and durable machine quilting. Next, consider whether or not time is a factor. Hand-quilting is perfect for the project with no deadline. Machine quilting is much faster and it's possible to machine quilt an entire project in a day of steady work. Lastly, consider the enjoyment you will (or won't) get from doing the quilting yourself. If you just don't like the quilting process—or if your schedule is overbooked with other activities—a machine quilting service may be just right for you and your quilt.

Binding

1. After quilting, trim excess batting and backing even with the edge of the quilt top. A rotary cutter and long ruler will ensure accurate straight edges. If basting is no longer in place, baste all three layers of the quilt together close to the edge.

2. Cut binding strips 2½" wide, either with the straight grain of the fabric or on the bias. Join the strips together using diagonal seams as shown. Make enough continuous binding to go around the four sides of the quilt plus 6" to 10" for overlap.

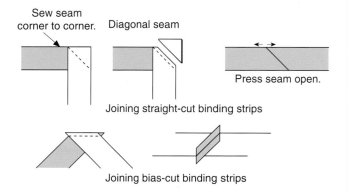

Sew seam corner to corner.   Diagonal seam

Press seam open.

Joining straight-cut binding strips

Joining bias-cut binding strips

3. Fold the binding in half lengthwise with wrong sides together and press, taking care not to stretch it. At one end, open out the fold and turn the raw edge in at a 45° angle. Press. Trim, leaving a ¼" seam allowance.

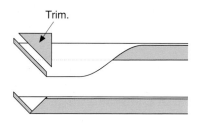

Trim.

4. Beginning on one edge of the quilt a few inches from a corner, pin the binding to the quilt top. Beginning two inches from the folded end of the binding, stitch ⅜" from the raw edges and stop ⅜" from the raw edge at the corner. Backstitch and remove the quilt.

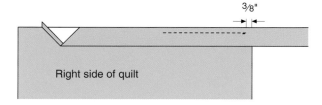

3/8"

Right side of quilt

5. Fold the binding back on itself to create a 45° angle, then turn the binding down to make a fold in the binding that is in line with the upper raw edge of the quilt top. Pin. Stitch the binding to the quilt, ending ⅜" from the next corner. Backstitch and miter the corner as you did the previous one.

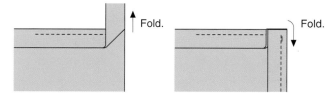

Fold.   Fold.

6. Continue in this manner until the binding has been stitched to all four edges of the quilt top. When you reach the beginning of the binding, trim away excess, leaving 1" to tuck into the folded binding. Complete the stitching.

7. Turn the binding to the back of the quilt and hand sew in place, mitering corners as shown.

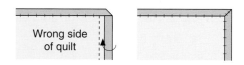

Wrong side of quilt

Arabesque

*T*he use of large prints and florals is important to achieve the elegance required to replicate the look of early 19th century quilts. Notice how Jackie spaced her luxurious floral print in the alternate blocks. She did not center the bouquets, but chose to cut her fabric selectively so stems and tendrils seem to be trailing into the adjacent areas. Select a large, clear or semi-transparent piece of template plastic and cut it the size of the finished block plus seam allowance. Lay your fabric out and place the plastic over it, parallel to selvage edge. Move the plastic template around the floral designs until you find a pattern you like. Using a pencil or marking pen, draw around the template. Keep the pattern on the straight of grain, so you will not have the difficulty of working with a stretchy bias. Cut on the marked lines and place squares on a design wall where you can begin to try out companion fabrics.

Jackie found many interesting fabrics in her stash, including the green William Morris reproduction print from Liberty of London®. The fabric is a light-weight wool and works beautifully. Notice the inner border and bits in the quilt composed of a rich leopard print. The spotted wildcat texture adds intrigue and a touch of exotica.

Arabesque

DESIGNED BY: **Jackie Quinn**   QUILTED BY: **Sherry Rogers**
FINISHED SIZE: **60¾" x 60¾"**   FINISHED BLOCK SIZE: **9" x 9"**

MATERIALS

Fabric requirements are based on 40" fabric width.

- 2 yds. floral bouquet print for outer border
- ⅓ yd. large floral for setting squares
- 10 or more assorted fat quarters for blocks
- ¾ yd. red two-tone print for sashing
- ⅞ yd. green two-tone print for side- and corner-setting triangles
- ½ yd. small floral print for first border
- ⅓ yd. leopard print for second border
- ⅔ yd. for binding
- 4⅛ yds. for backing
- 69" x 69" batting

DIRECTIONS

Read these instructions thoroughly before starting. It's important to understand the whole process before you begin. Because the setting pieces and borders are so important to the overall design, you may want to cut them and place them in position on your design wall before making the Ohio Trail blocks. See *Basic Quiltmaking Techniques*, beginning on page 24, for general quiltmaking directions. All cutting measurements include ¼"-wide seam allowance.

Ohio Trail Blocks

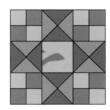

9" Block

Cutting

From assorted fat quarters, cut:

- 18 strips, 2" x 20+", for Fourpatch units (2 strips for each block)
- 18 squares, 4¼" x 4¼", for star points (2 for each block)
- 18 squares, 4¼" x 4¼", for background of star points (2 for each block)
- 9 squares, 3½" x 3½", for star centers (1 for each block)

Assembly

1. Make 36 Fourpatch units, 4 for each block. Using 18 strips, 2" x 20+", make 9 strip units (1 strip unit for each block). Press seams toward darker fabric. From each strip unit, crosscut a total of 8 segments, each 2" wide.

2"

Make 9 strip units.
Cut 8 segments from each strip unit (72 total).

Arrange the segments in pairs and join together to make Fourpatch units. Press seams to one side. Check completed units to make sure they measure 3½" x 3½" (cut edge to cut edge).

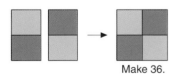

Make 36.

Fabric Selection Tips

Jackie selectively cut the small centers of her blocks using floral details from the border and focus fabric. She took advantage of the transparency of the Precision Trimmer 3™ to find interesting parts of fruits and flowers to highlight.

2. Make 36 half-square triangle units, 4 for each block. For each block, choose 2 accent squares, 4¼" x 4¼", for star points; and 2 squares, 4¼" x 4¼", for backgrounds. With right sides together, arrange the squares in pairs; one accent, one background. Working with one pair of squares at a time, make a cut diagonally, corner to corner, yielding 2 pairs of triangles. Stitching the long side, sew each triangle pair together with ¼" seams. Press seams toward the darker fabric. Check completed unit to make sure it measures 3⅞" x 3⅞" (cut edge to cut edge).

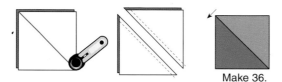

Make 36.

3. Make 36 quarter-square triangle units for star points, 4 for each block. Match pairs of half-square triangle units, right sides together, nesting opposing seams. Cut squares diagonally and sew resulting triangle pairs together with ¼" seams. Press seams to one side. Check completed unit to make sure it measures 3½" x 3½" (cut edge to cut edge).

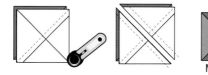

Make 36.

4. Join the Fourpatch units, quarter-square triangle units, and 3½" squares together in rows. Press for opposing seams. Sew rows together to complete each block. Press seams to one side.

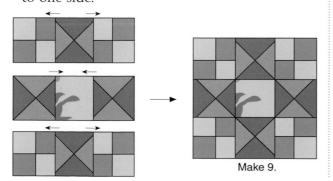

Make 9.

Sashing and Setting Pieces
Cutting
From red two-tone print, cut:
- 3 strips; cut strips the width of fabric, 2" x 40", for Sashing Strip D
- 2 strips, 2" x 33½", for Sashing Strip C
- 2 strips, 2" x 12½", for Sashing Strip B
- 18 strips, 2" x 9½", for Sashing Strip A

From large floral, cut:
- 4 squares, 9½" x 9½", for setting squares

From green two-tone print, cut:
- 2 squares, 16⅛" x 16⅛"; cut each square twice diagonally to make 8 side-setting triangles
- 2 squares, 9⅜" x 9⅜"; cut each square once diagonally to make 4 corner-setting triangles

Assembly
1. Sew the three 2" x 40" strips together end-to-end. Press seams open. From the long strip, cut 2 Sashing Strips D, each 2" x 54½".
2. Sew a Sashing Strip A to opposite sides of each Ohio Trail block as shown in the Quilt Assembly Diagram on page 37. Press seams toward sashing strips.
3. Join the Ohio Trail/Strip A blocks, and the setting squares, together in rows. Press seams toward setting squares.
4. Sew the Sashing Strips B, C, and D to the block rows as shown in the Quilt Assembly Diagram. Press seams toward sashing strips.
5. Join side- and corner-setting triangles to the block rows. Press seams to one side. Sew rows together.

Borders

Cutting

From small floral print, cut:
- 6 strips, 2" x 40", for first border

From leopard print, cut:
- 6 strips, 1¼" x 40", for second border

From floral bouquet print, cut:
- 4 strips the length of the fabric x 5" wide, for outer border (Strips are cut longer than necessary and will be trimmed to size later.)

Assembly

1. Sew the 6 small-floral strips together, end-to-end, to make one long strip. Press seams open.

2. Measure length of quilt through center. Cut 2 small-floral border strips (from the long strip) to this measurement, and sew to sides of quilt top. Press seams toward border.

3. Measure width of quilt, including borders just added, through center. Cut 2 small-floral border strips (from the long strip) to this measurement, and sew to top and bottom of quilt. Press seams toward border.

4. Sew the 6 leopard print strips together, end-to-end, to make one long strip. Press seams open. Following general instructions in Steps 2 and 3 above, add the second border. Sew side borders first, then top and bottom. Press seams toward first border.

5. Place 2 of the floral bouquet border strips next to the sides of your quilt top, and decide on the placement of the floral bouquets. Measure length of quilt through center. Trim the 2 floral bouquet strips to this measurement, and sew to sides of quilt top. Press seams toward outer border.

6. Measure width of quilt, including borders just added, through center. Arrange and trim remaining 2 floral bouquet strips to this measurement, and sew to top and bottom of quilt. Press seams toward outer border.

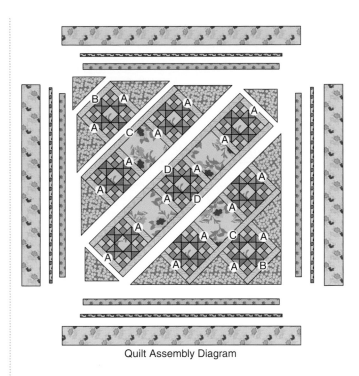

Quilt Assembly Diagram

Finishing

1. Cut the backing fabric into two equal lengths and sew long edges together. Press seam open. Trim backing to 69" x 69".

2. Plan and mark quilting design as desired.

3. Layer quilt top, batting, and backing. Baste layers together.

4. Quilt by hand or machine.

5. Trim the batting and backing even with the quilt top edges.

6. Make and apply binding. From binding fabric, cut enough strips (each 2½" wide) either across the width of fabric, or across the bias, to make 260" of continuous binding. Bind the quilt edges.

7. Add a hanging sleeve if desired. Sign and date your finished quilt.

Chintz Variable Star

$\mathcal{T}$his quilt is an example of
experimentation with value. Study the twenty star blocks
and see how Marsha used color mixtures so close in value that
some stars almost disappear. Notice how the fabrics blend in
the lower right hand corner and some of the stars appear to
float. There is no right or wrong in these blocks. You are free
to do what pleases you. Work on your design wall until
you create a rich tapestry of texture and color. You will be
delighted to discover your inner artist.

This star seems to disappear as an area of rich texture is created with the use of similar-value prints.

Chintz Variable Star

DESIGNED BY: **Marsha McCloskey**   QUILTED BY: **Virginia Lauth**

FINISHED SIZE: **70½" x 83"**   FINISHED BLOCK SIZE: **9" x 9"**

MATERIALS

Fabric requirements are based on 40" fabric width.

- 3¼ yds. large floral (dark) for set pieces and outer border (Fabric A)
- ¾ yd. large floral (medium) for set pieces (Fabric B)
- ¾ yd. large floral (light) for set pieces (Fabric C)
- ⅔ yd. dark print for inner border
- 12 or more assorted fat quarters for blocks
- ¾ yd. for binding
- 5½ yds. for backing
- 79" x 91" batting

DIRECTIONS

Read these instructions thoroughly before starting. It's important to understand the whole process before you begin. Because the setting pieces and borders are so important to the overall design, you may want to cut them and place them in position on your design wall before making the Variable Star blocks. See *Basic Quiltmaking Techniques*, beginning on page 24, for general quiltmaking directions. All cutting measurements include ¼"-wide seam allowance.

Variable Star Blocks

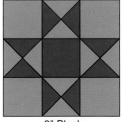

9" Block

Cutting instructions are given for all 20 Variable Star blocks, but this is a scrappy treatment, and you may want to cut only enough patches for one block at a time.

Cutting

From assorted fat quarters, cut:

- 40 squares, 4¼" x 4¼", dark or accent color for star points (2 for each block)
- 40 squares, 4¼" x 4¼", for background of star points (2 for each block)
- 20 squares, 3½" x 3½", dark or accent colors for star centers (1 for each block)
- 80 squares, 3½" x 3½", background for star corners (4 for each block)

Assembly

1. Make 80 half-square triangle units, 4 for each block. For each block, choose 2 accent squares, 4¼" x 4¼", for star points; and 2 squares, 4¼" x 4¼", for backgrounds. With right sides together, arrange the squares in pairs; one accent, one background. Working with one pair of squares at a time, make a cut diagonally, corner to corner, yielding 2 pairs of triangles. Stitching the long side, sew each triangle pair together with ¼" seams. Press seams toward the darker fabric. Check completed unit to make sure it measures 3⅞" x 3⅞" (cut edge to cut edge).

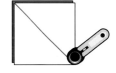

Make 80.

Fabric Selection Tips

Marsha built an area around the six inner stars to emphasize the contrast of dark and medium fabrics and to create an outline. Notice how the outline almost disappears in the upper right hand corner because the medium and dark fabrics were cut with dense florals that blend. Choose fabrics with different background colors but similar floral colors that fuse into each other.

2. Make 80 quarter-square triangle units for star points, 4 for each block. Match pairs of half-square triangle units, right sides together, nesting opposing seams. Cut squares diagonally and sew resulting triangle pairs together with ¼" seams. Press seams to one side. Check completed unit to make sure it measures 3½" x 3½" (cut edge to cut edge).

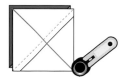

Make 80.

3. Piece each Variable Star block, joining the 3½" squares and the quarter-square triangle units in rows. Press seams toward 3½" squares. Join the rows. Press seams to one side.

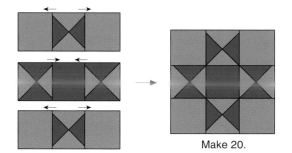

Make 20.

Precision Cutting

Use Marsha McCloskey's Precision Trimmer 3™ to check your work. Position the ruler on the pieced unit as shown, and trim the edges to make perfect 3½" squares.

Using the Precision Trimmer 3™
to true-up pieced squares

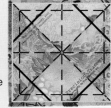

Quarter-square
Triangle Unit

Setting Pieces
Cutting

Fabric A. This fabric is used for both the border and outer setting triangles. Cut the border strips first and set them aside; then cut the setting triangles.

From large floral (dark), cut:
- 4 lengthwise strips, 8" x 80", for outer border (Strips are cut longer than necessary and will be trimmed to size later.)
- 4 squares, 14" x 14"; cut each square twice diagonally to make 16 side-setting triangles (2 extra)
- 2 squares, 7¼" x 7¼"; cut each square once diagonally to make 4 corner-setting triangles

Fabric B. From large floral (medium), cut:
- 5 squares, 9⅞" x 9⅞"; cut each square once diagonally to make 10 triangles
- 1 square, 10¼" x 10¼"; cut square twice diagonally to make 4 triangles

Fabric C. From large floral (light), cut:
- 2 squares, 9½" x 9½", for setting squares
- 3 squares, 9⅞" x 9⅞"; cut each square once diagonally to make 6 triangles
- 1 square, 10¼" x 10¼"; cut square twice diagonally to make 4 triangles

Assembly

Join Variable Star blocks with setting pieces in diagonal rows, paying close attention to the Quilt Assembly Diagram on page 43 for placement of light, medium, and dark setting pieces. In some places, it will be necessary to sew setting triangles together to form squares before making the diagonal rows. Press for opposing seams from row to row. Sew diagonal rows together.

Borders

Cutting

From dark print, cut:

- 8 strips, 2½" x 40", for inner border

Assembly

1. Sew the 2½"-wide inner border strips together, end-to-end, in pairs to make 4 strips, 2½" x 80".
2. Measure length of the quilt through center. Trim 2 of the 2½"-wide strips to size, and sew to sides of quilt top. Press seams toward border.
3. Measure width of quilt, including borders just added, through center. Trim remaining 2½"-wide strips to size, and sew to top and bottom of quilt. Press seams toward border.
4. Following general instructions in Steps 2 and 3 above, add the 8"-wide outer border strips cut from Fabric A. Sew side borders first, then top and bottom.

Finishing

1. Cut the backing fabric into two equal lengths and sew long edges together. Press seam open. Trim backing to 79" x 91".
2. Plan and mark quilting design as desired.
3. Layer quilt top, batting, and backing. Baste layers together.
4. Quilt by hand or machine.
5. Trim the batting and backing even with the quilt top edges.

Quilt Assembly Diagram

6. Make and apply binding. From binding fabric, cut enough strips (each 2½" wide) either across the width of fabric, or across the bias, to make 324" of continuous binding. Bind the quilt edges.
7. Add a hanging sleeve if desired. Sign and date your finished quilt.

Parisian Garden

$\mathcal{M}$arsha used many small blue prints in the pieced-border triangles. These are areas of rest where florals would have been too busy. Your design may flow beautifully but you need to know when to stop or you will have a quilt that is too busy. Monochromatic colorways work well here to form visual resting places. Think close shades of gold, beige, green, or blue. Small to medium tone-on-tones or large, subtle designs mix well. Pull a color from your large floral and find fabrics that blend. You will want to find some lighter and darker pieces to add interest.

Parisian Garden

DESIGNED BY: **Marsha McCloskey**   QUILTED BY: **Gem Taylor**

FINISHED SIZE: **61¾" x 61¾"**   FINISHED CENTER BLOCK SIZE: **17" x 17"**

The combination of toile and several floral prints flow into each other. The color red is a common link allowing your eye to read a graceful blending of flowers.

MATERIALS

Fabric requirements are based on 40" fabric width.

- 1⅛ yds. red toile for center square and pieced borders
- ⅔ yd. yellow floral bouquet print for triangles around center square, and pieced borders
- 8 or more assorted blue fat quarters for pieced borders
- 4 or more assorted yellow fat quarters for pieced borders
- 1¾ yds. medium-size yellow floral print for plain borders
- ¼ yd. medium-size green floral print for pieced borders
- 1¾ yds. floral stripe for outer border
- ⅔ yd. for binding
- 4¼ yds. for backing
- 70" x 70" batting

DIRECTIONS

Read these instructions thoroughly before starting. See *Basic Quiltmaking Techniques*, beginning on page 24, for general quiltmaking directions. All cutting measurements include ¼"-wide seam allowance.

Center Block
Cutting

From red toile, cut:
- 1 square, 12½" x 12½", for Square A

From yellow floral bouquet print, cut:
- 2 squares, 9⅜" x 9⅜"; cut each square once diagonally to make 4 Triangles B

Assembly

Join 4 Triangles B to Square A as pictured. Press seams toward triangles.

Center Block

Chain of Squares Border
Cutting

From red toile, cut:
- 52 squares, 3½" x 3½", for Squares C (20 squares will be used for this border; set the other 32 aside to use in the Fourpatch Border)

From assorted blue fat quarters, cut:
- 11 squares, 5½" x 5½"; cut each square twice diagonally to make 44 Triangles D (20 triangles will be used for this border; set the other 24 aside to use in the Dogtooth Border)
- 2 squares, 3" x 3"; cut each square once diagonally to make 4 Triangles E

From assorted yellow fat quarters, cut:
- 4 squares, 5½" x 5½"; cut each square twice diagonally to make 16 Triangles D
- 2 squares, 3" x 3"; cut each square once diagonally to make 4 Triangles E

Fabric Selection Tips

The red toile was chosen for the center square because it is so gorgeous in an uncut larger piece. (Actually, the center square for this quilt design could be any pieced or appliquéd block that measures 12" finished.) The red toile and red-and-yellow florals were chosen first. The blues are keyed to color elements in the other prints.

Trimming Points for Easy Matching

The Precision Trimmer 3™ is designed to trim points on 45° angle patches. Use it to trim points on the D, E, and F triangles in the Chain of Squares and Dogtooth borders. Position the ruler on the triangles as shown. The points of the triangle will stick out ⅜". Trim them off with the rotary cutter. This takes the guesswork out of matching the cut patches before stitching.

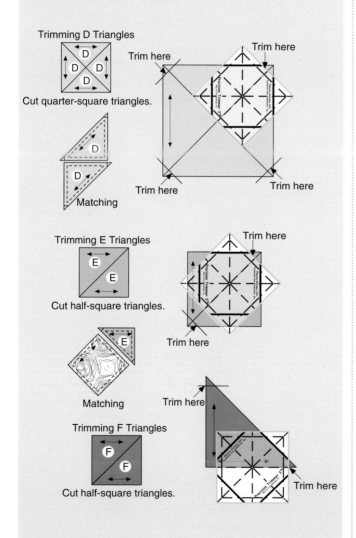

Trimming D Triangles

Cut quarter-square triangles.

Matching

Trim here

Trim here

Trim here

Trim here

Trimming E Triangles

Cut half-square triangles.

Matching

Trim here

Trim here

Trimming F Triangles

Cut half-square triangles.

Trim here

Trim here

Assembly

1. Following the illustrations below, make 2 of Border Unit I, 2 of Border Unit II, and 4 of the Corner Unit. Press seams toward triangles.

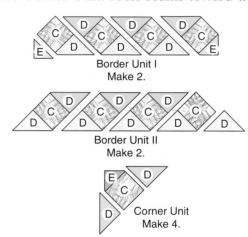

Border Unit I
Make 2.

Border Unit II
Make 2.

Corner Unit
Make 4.

2. Sew the 2 Border Units I to opposite sides of the Center block. Press seams toward Center block. Sew the 2 Border Units II to the top and bottom of the Center block. Press seams toward the Center block. Join the 4 Corner Units to corners of the border. Press seams to one side.

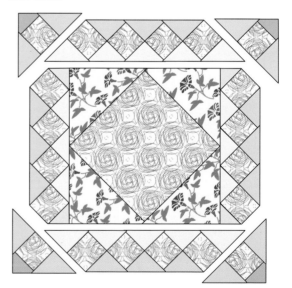

Dogtooth Border

Cutting

From medium-size green floral print, cut:

- 5 squares, 5½" x 5½"; cut each square twice diagonally to make 20 Triangles D
- 2 squares, 5⅛" x 5⅛"; cut each square once diagonally to make 4 Triangles F

Assembly

1. Using 20 green floral print Triangles D and 24 assorted blue Triangles D (cut previously), make 4 Dogtooth Border units as pictured.

Make 4.

2. Join a Dogtooth Border unit to each side of the quilt center. Press seams to one side. Sew a green floral print Triangle F to each corner. Press seams toward triangles.

Plain Border #1

Cutting

From medium-size yellow floral print, cut:

- 4 lengthwise strips, 2⅝" x 31"

Assembly

1. Using the guideline on your acrylic ruler, cut a 45° angle at each end of the four 2⅝" x 31" border strips as pictured.

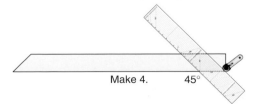

Make 4.　　45°

2. Sew 2 of the border strips to the sides of quilt as shown in the Quilt Assembly Diagram on page 51. Press seams toward plain border. Sew remaining 2 border strips to top and bottom of quilt. Press seams toward plain border.

Fourpatch Border

6" Block　　6" Block

Cutting

From yellow floral bouquet print, cut:

- 3 squares, 9¾" x 9¾"; cut each square twice diagonally to make 12 side-setting Triangles G
- 2 squares, 5⅛" x 5⅛"; cut each square once diagonally to make 4 corner-setting Triangles H

From assorted blue fat quarters, cut:

- 5 squares, 9¾" x 9¾"; cut each square twice diagonally to make 20 side-setting Triangles G
- 7 strips, 2" x 20+", for Fourpatch units
- 18 squares, 4¼" x 4¼", for Yankee Puzzle blocks

From assorted yellow fat quarters, cut:

- 7 strips, 2" x 20+", for Fourpatch units
- 10 squares, 4¼" x 4¼", for Yankee Puzzle blocks

From red toile, cut:

- 8 squares, 4¼" x 4¼", for Yankee Puzzle blocks

Double Fourpatch Block Assembly

1. Make 32 Fourpatch units, 2 for each block. Using 7 blue strips, 2" x 20+", and 7 yellow strips, 2" x 20+", make 7 strip units. Press seams toward blue fabrics. Crosscut a total of 64 segments, each 2" wide.

2"

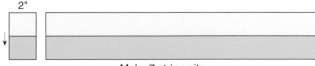

Make 7 strip units.
Cut 64 segments.

Arrange the segments in pairs and sew together to make Fourpatch units. Press seams to one side. Check completed units to make sure they measure 3½" x 3½" (cut edge to cut edge).

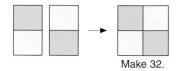

Make 32.

2. Use the 3½" red toile squares set aside earlier, and sew 1 Fourpatch unit to 1 red toile Square C. Press seam toward square. Make 32 of these Fourpatch/C units.

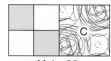

Make 32.

3. Matching opposing seams, sew together Fourpatch/C units in pairs to complete Double Fourpatch blocks.

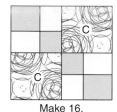

Make 16.

Yankee Puzzle Block Assembly

1. Make 36 half-square triangle units. With right sides together, arrange the 4¼" x 4¼" squares in pairs. Make sure that there is a blue square in each pair. The remaining square in each pair will be either a yellow print or red toile. Working with one pair of squares at a time, make a cut diagonally, corner to corner, yielding 2 pairs of triangles. Stitching the long side, sew each triangle pair together with ¼" seams. Press seams to one side. Check completed unit to make sure it measures 3⅞" x 3⅞" (cut edge to cut edge).

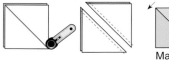

Make 36.

2. Make 36 quarter-square triangle units. Match pairs of half-square triangle units, right sides together, nesting opposing seams. Cut squares diagonally and sew resulting triangle pairs together with ¼" seams. Press seams to one side. Check completed unit to make sure it measures 3½" x 3½" (cut edge to cut edge). Set aside 4 of the blue/yellow quarter-square triangle units to be used in outer border.

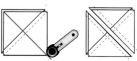

Make 36.
Set aside 4.

3. Sew 32 quarter-square triangle units together in pairs, and then blocks as shown. Press seams to one side.

Make 16.

Make 8.

Fourpatch Border Assembly

1. Make 4 Fourpatch Border Side Units as pictured. For each use 2 Double Fourpatch blocks, 3 yellow floral bouquet print Triangles G, and 1 blue print Triangle G.

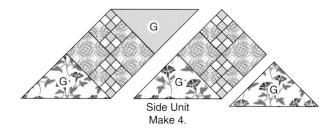

Side Unit
Make 4.

2. Make 4 Fourpatch Border Corner Units as pictured. For each use 2 Double Fourpatch blocks, 2 Yankee Puzzle blocks, 4 blue print Triangles G, and 1 yellow floral bouquet Triangle H.

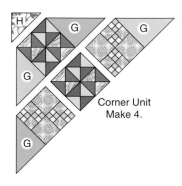

Corner Unit
Make 4.

3. Sew Side Units and Corner Units to quilt as shown in the Quilt Assembly Diagram on this page. Press Side Unit seams toward plain border. Press Corner Unit seams to one side.

Plain Border #2
Cutting
From medium-size yellow floral print, cut:
- 4 strips the length of the fabric x $2\frac{5}{8}$" wide (Strips are cut longer than necessary and will be trimmed to size later.)

Assembly
1. Measure length of quilt through center. Trim 2 of the $2\frac{5}{8}$"-wide border strips to this measurement, and sew to sides of quilt. Press seams toward plain border.
2. Measure width of quilt, including borders just added, through center. Trim remaining $2\frac{5}{8}$"-wide border strips to this measurement, and sew to top and bottom of quilt. Press seams toward plain border.

Outer Border
Cutting
From floral stripe, cut:
- 4 strips the length of the fabric x $3\frac{1}{2}$" wide (Strips are cut longer than necessary and will be trimmed to size later.)

Assembly
1. Measure width of quilt through center. Trim 2 of the $3\frac{1}{2}$"-wide border strips to this measurement. Sew 2 blue-and-yellow quarter-square triangle units to opposite ends of the border strip. Press seams toward strip. Make 2 of these pieced border strips.
2. Measure length of quilt through center. Trim remaining $3\frac{1}{2}$"-wide border strips to this measurement, and sew to sides of quilt top. Press seams toward outer border.
3. Sew 2 pieced border strips to top and bottom of quilt. Press seams to one side.

Finishing
1. Cut the backing fabric into two equal lengths and sew long edges together. Press seam open. Trim backing to 70" x 70".
2. Plan and mark quilting design as desired.
3. Layer quilt top, batting, and backing. Baste layers together.
4. Quilt by hand or machine.
5. Trim the batting and backing even with the quilt top edges.
6. Make and apply binding. From binding fabric, cut enough strips (each $2\frac{1}{2}$" wide) either across the width of fabric, or across the bias, to make 264" of continuous binding. Bind the quilt edges.
7. Add a hanging sleeve if desired. Sign and date your finished quilt.

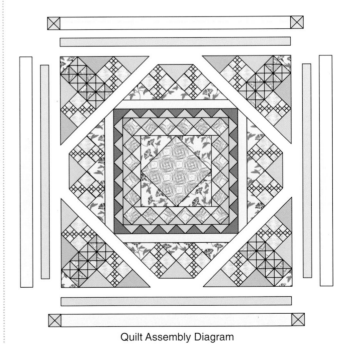

Quilt Assembly Diagram

*C*athy created this quilt with elegant floral fabrics reminiscent of the early 1800s. She used a center medallion or frame format similar to quilts of that era. Notice her use of simple shapes and large areas to showcase large-scale prints. By using many fabrics of beige and gray she created a mellow, antique mood.

With the medallion design, it is easiest to start with the center fabric and work outward. Once you determine the colors in the center piece, you can create the star blocks to blend or contrast. Cathy placed the star blocks in uneven borders just because she wanted to! In the early 19th century, limited fabric choices meant that women often needed to put aside specific rules of evenness, balance, or color when making their quilts. They were free to use their artistic skills and enjoy their creativity. It's the 21st century. Have we made progress? Go for it!

Areas contain elements of low contrast which allow for luxurious textures. Beige, gray, and brown permit the addition of deep rich colors for a vintage look.

Simple Gifts

DESIGNED BY: **Cathy Mathes**   QUILTED BY: **Becky Kraus**
FINISHED SIZE: **69" x 69"**   FINISHED CENTER SQUARE: **9" x 9"**
FINISHED BLOCK SIZE: **9" x 9"**

MATERIALS

Fabric requirements are based on 40" fabric width.

- 18 or more assorted fat quarters for blocks
- ¾ yd. dark toile for corner-setting triangles and blocks
- ¾ yd. medium-scale dark floral print for Medallion border
- 1¾ yds. light floral bouquet print for outer border
- ¾ yd. for binding
- 4⅝ yds. for backing
- 77" x 77" batting

DIRECTIONS

Read these instructions thoroughly before starting. It's important to understand the whole process before you begin. See *Basic Quiltmaking Techniques*, beginning on page 24, for general quiltmaking directions. All cutting measurements include ¼"-wide seam allowance.

Center Medallion

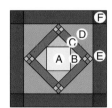

Cutting

From assorted fat quarters, cut:

- 1 square, 9½" x 9½", for center Square A
- 2 squares, 7¼" x 7¼"; cut squares once diagonally to make 4 Triangles B
- 4 rectangles, 3½" x 13¼", for Rectangles C
- 2 strips, 2" x 20+", for Fourpatch units (use 2 different prints for your strips)
- 4 squares, 5¼" x 5¼", for Squares F

From dark toile, cut:

- 2 squares, 14⅛" x 14⅛"; cut each square once diagonally to make 4 Triangles D

From medium-scale dark floral print, cut:

- 4 strips, 5¼" x 27", for Rectangles E

Assembly

1. Sew 4 Triangles B to center Square A. Press seams toward triangles.

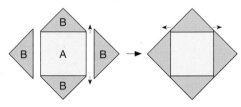

2. Make 4 Fourpatch units. Using 2 strips, 2" x 20+", make 1 strip unit. Press seam toward darker fabric. Crosscut a total of 8 segments, each 2" wide.

Make 1 strip unit.
Cut 8 segments.

Arrange the segments in pairs and sew together to make Fourpatch units. Press seams to one side. Check completed units to make sure they measure 3½" x 3½" (cut edge to cut edge).

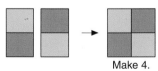

Make 4.

3. Sew 2 Rectangles C to opposite sides of block. Press seams toward rectangles. Sew 4 Fourpatch units to opposite sides of

Fabric Selection Tips

When choosing your fat quarters, look for two or three large floral prints, and a focal print that features a scene appropriate for the center of the Medallion. You may need to buy yardage, rather than fat quarters, for some of these pieces. In that case, determine your fabric requirements based on the particular piece of fabric. You may need to buy a half-yard cut to get the design you need. Round out your fat quarter selections by choosing some smaller florals, and several tone-on-tone prints.

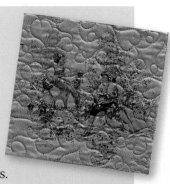

remaining 2 Rectangles C. Press seams toward rectangles. Sew 2 Fourpatch/Rectangle C units to remaining sides of block. Press seams toward Fourpatch/Rectangle C units.

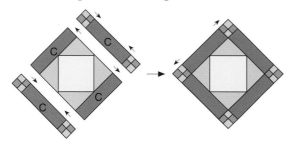

4. Sew 4 Triangles D to block. Press seams toward triangles.

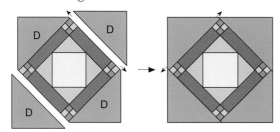

5. Sew 2 Rectangles E to opposite sides of block. Press seams toward rectangles. Sew 4 Squares F to ends of remaining 2 Rectangles E. Press seams toward rectangles. Sew the resulting strips to top and bottom of block. Press seams toward strips. Check to make sure that your completed center Medallion measures 36½" x 36½".

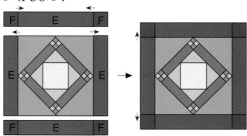

Star Border

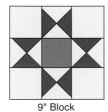

9" Block

Cutting instructions are given for all 10 Variable Star blocks, but this is a scrappy treatment, and you may want to cut only enough patches for one block at a time. Each block will give you ideas for the next.

Cutting
From assorted fat quarters, cut:
- 10 squares, 9½" x 9½", for alternate blocks in Star Border (if desired, you can cut 1 or more of these 10 squares from the dark toile)
- 20 squares, 4¼" x 4¼", dark or accent color for star points (2 for each Variable Star block)
- 20 squares, 4¼" x 4¼", for background of star points (2 for each Variable Star block)
- 10 squares, 3½" x 3½", dark or accent colors for star centers (1 for each Variable Star block)
- 40 squares, 3½" x 3½", background for star corners (4 for each Variable Star block)

Variable Star Block Assembly
1. Make 40 half-square triangle units, 4 for each block. For each block, choose 2 accent squares, 4¼" x 4¼", for star points; and 2 squares, 4¼" x 4¼", for backgrounds. With right sides together, arrange the squares in pairs; one accent, one background. Working with one pair of squares at a time, make a cut diagonally, corner to corner, yielding 2 pairs of triangles. Stitching the long side, sew each triangle pair together with ¼" seams. Press seams toward the darker fabric. Check completed unit to make sure it measures 3⅞" x 3⅞" (cut edge to cut edge).

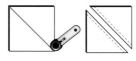

Make 40.

2. Make 40 quarter-square triangle units for star points, 4 for each block. Match pairs of half-square triangle units, right sides together, nesting opposing seams. Cut squares diagonally and sew resulting triangle pairs together with ¼" seams. Press seams to one side. Check completed unit to make sure it measures 3½" x 3½" (cut edge to cut edge).

Make 40.

3. Piece each Variable Star block, joining the 3½" squares and the quarter-square triangle units together in rows. Press seams toward 3½" squares. Join the rows. Press seams to one side.

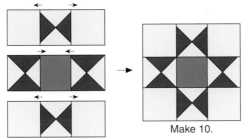

Make 10.

Star Border Assembly

1. Sew the 10 Variable Star blocks and 10 alternate blocks together in 4 border strips as shown. Press seams in direction of arrows.

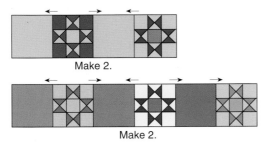

Make 2.

Make 2.

2. As shown in the Quilt Assembly Diagram at right, sew the 4-block border strips to sides of the Medallion. Press seams toward Medallion. Sew the 6-block border strips to top and bottom of the Medallion. Press seams toward Medallion.

Outer Border

Cutting

From assorted fat quarters, cut:
- 2 squares, 5½" x 5½", for Squares G
- 8 squares, 4⁷⁄₁₆" x 4⁷⁄₁₆"; cut each square once diagonally to make 16 Triangles H

From dark toile, cut:
- 2 squares, 5½" x 5½", for Squares G

From light floral bouquet print, cut:
- 4 lengthwise strips, 7½" x 54½", for outer border

Assembly

1. Sew 2 floral bouquet border strips to sides of quilt top.

2. Piece 4 Square-in-a-Square corner blocks using 4 Squares G and 16 Triangles H. Press seams toward triangles.

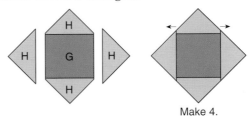

Make 4.

3. Sew Square-in-a-Square corner blocks to ends of remaining 2 floral bouquet border strips. Press seams toward strips. Sew these Square-in-a-Square border strips to top and bottom of quilt top. Press seams toward borders.

Finishing

1. Cut the backing fabric into two equal lengths and sew long edges together. Press seam open. Trim backing to 77" x 77".
2. Plan and mark quilting design as desired.
3. Layer quilt top, batting, and backing. Baste layers together.
4. Quilt by hand or machine.
5. Trim the batting and backing even with the quilt top edges.
6. Make and apply binding. From binding fabric, cut enough strips (each 2½" wide) either across the width of fabric, or across the bias, to make 292" of continuous binding. Bind the quilt edges.
7. Add a hanging sleeve if desired. Sign and date your finished quilt.

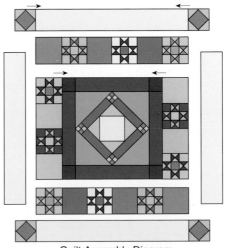

Quilt Assembly Diagram

Garden Steps

$\mathcal{M}$arsha's pretty quilt is a variation
of the traditional "Courthouse Steps" pattern. Notice how she
has used splashes of color to relate one fabric to another and
disguise the seam lines. Blocks with more definition are spread
randomly throughout the quilt. The top and side blocks are
purposely in light to medium values to blend with the lush toile
in the border. You might eliminate the dark blocks and spread
more small triangles throughout, or how about more dark blocks
to create an exciting, intense piece. It's up to you. Use your own
ingenuity and watch your quilt designs grow!

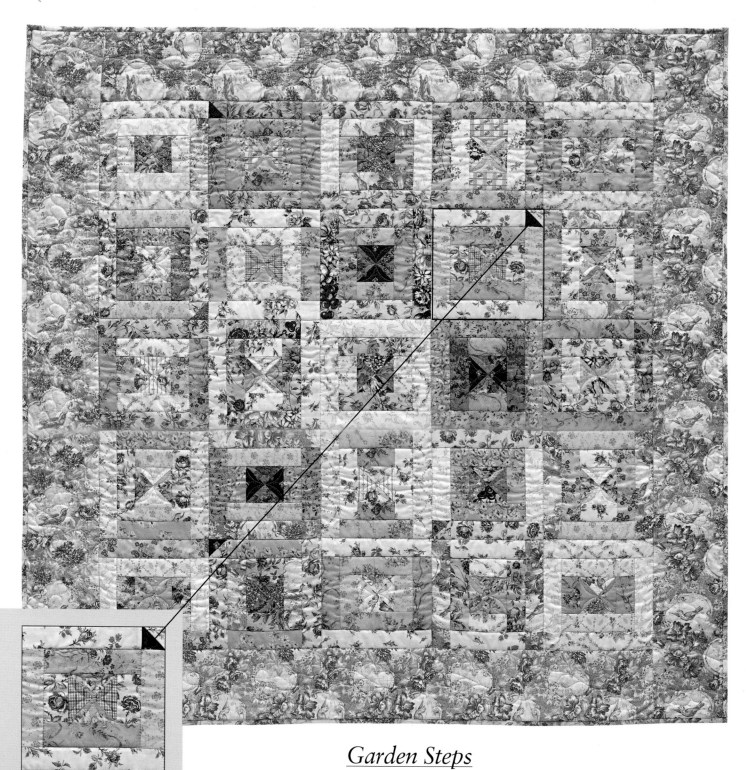

A group of fabrics shift color gradually in a soft blend punctuated by a deep-colored sparkling triangle.

Garden Steps

DESIGNED BY: **Marsha McCloskey**   QUILTED BY: **Gretchen Engle**
FINISHED SIZE: **57½" x 57½"**   FINISHED BLOCK SIZE: **9" x 9"**

MATERIALS

Fabric requirements are based on 40" fabric width.

- 1⅞ yds. pink toile for border
- 12 or more assorted fat quarters—mostly pastels and light-value prints
- ⅝ yd. for binding
- 4 yds. for backing
- 66" x 66" batting

DIRECTIONS

Read these instructions thoroughly before starting. See *Basic Quiltmaking Techniques*, beginning on page 24, for general quiltmaking directions. All cutting measurements include ¼"-wide seam allowance.

Garden Steps Blocks

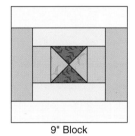

9" Block

Cutting instructions are given for all 25 Garden Steps blocks, but this is a scrappy treatment, and you may want to cut only a few patches at a time. It's fun to make fabric decisions as you go, and to see the overall quilt design grow on the design wall.

Cutting

From assorted fat quarters, cut:

- 26 squares, 4¼" x 4¼", for quarter-square triangle units
- At least 84* strips, 2" x 17+" (cut strips parallel to selvage); crosscut
  - 50 short rectangles, 2" x 3½", for "steps"
  - 100 medium rectangles, 2" x 6½", for "steps"
  - 50 long rectangles, 2" x 9½", for "steps"
  *For more variety (and more options when you reach the piecing stage), cut additional strips from different fabrics.

Block Assembly

1. Make 26 half-square triangle units. With right sides together, arrange the 4¼" squares in pairs. Working with one pair of squares at a time, make a cut diagonally, corner to corner, yielding 2 pairs of triangles. Stitching the long side, sew each triangle pair together with ¼" seams. Press seams to one side. Check completed unit to make sure it measures 3⅞" x 3⅞" (cut edge to cut edge).

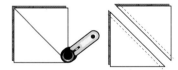

Make 26.

Fabric Selection Tips

The Garden Steps quilt features 25 different fabrics—some in very small amounts. Usually a motif in one fabric picks up a color in another fabric, or a motif color in one block becomes the background color in another block. Before buying larger cuts of accent fabrics, check your scrap bag for suitable pieces.

2. Make 26 quarter-square triangle units (there will be one extra). Match pairs of half-square triangle units, right sides together, nesting opposing seams. Cut squares diagonally and sew resulting triangle pairs together with ¼" seams. Press seams to one side. Check completed unit to make sure it measures 3½" x 3½" (cut edge to cut edge).

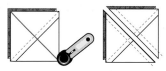

Make 26.

3. Sew 2 short rectangles to opposite sides of each quarter-square triangle unit. Press seams toward short rectangles. Add 2 medium rectangles to long sides of unit. Press seams toward medium rectangles. Add 2 more medium rectangles (of a different print) to opposite sides of unit. Press seams toward medium rectangles. Make 25 of these pieced units.

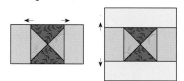

Make 25.

4. Before sewing long rectangles to your pieced units, decide if you'd like to add accent triangles to several rectangles. The sample quilt has 3 red and 3 blue accent triangles. For a similar effect, trim 6 of your long rectangles to measure 2" x 8".

Choose two accent fabrics and cut a total of 4 squares, 2⅜" x 2⅜". Cut each square once diagonally to make 8 accent triangles (2 leftover). Select the same 6 fabrics as used in your 2" x 8" rectangles, and cut one square, 2⅜" x 2⅜", from each fabric. Cut each square once diagonally to make 12 background triangles (6 leftover). Sew accent triangles and background triangles together in pairs. Press seams toward darker fabric.

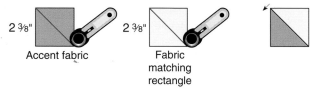

2⅜"   Accent fabric   2⅜"   Fabric matching rectangle

Sew one of these half-square triangle units to the end of each 2" x 8" rectangle. Press seams toward rectangles. In the following step, these accented rectangles will be treated the same as the long rectangles.

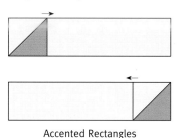

Accented Rectangles
Make 6.
(Place triangle accent as desired. Orientation may vary from one rectangle to another.)

5. Add 2 long rectangles to long sides of each pieced unit. Press seams toward long rectangles.

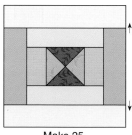

Make 25.

Quilt Top Assembly

Join blocks in rows as shown in the Quilt Assembly Diagram below. Notice that the orientation of the Garden Steps alternates from block to block. Sew rows together.

Border

Cutting

From pink toile, cut:

- 4 strips the length of the fabric x 6½" wide (Strips are cut longer than necessary and will be trimmed to size later.)

Assembly

1. Measure length of quilt through center. Trim 2 of the border strips to this measurement, and sew to sides of quilt top. Press seams toward border.
2. Measure width of quilt, including borders just added, through center. Trim remaining border strips to this measurement, and sew to top and bottom of quilt. Press seams toward border.

Finishing

1. Cut the backing fabric into two equal lengths and sew long edges together. Press seam open. Trim backing to 66" x 66".
2. Plan and mark quilting design as desired.
3. Layer quilt top, batting, and backing. Baste layers together.
4. Quilt by hand or machine.
5. Trim the batting and backing even with the quilt top edges.
6. Make and apply binding. From binding fabric, cut enough strips (each 2½" wide) either across the width of fabric, or across the bias, to make 248" of continuous binding. Bind the quilt edges.
7. Add a hanging sleeve if desired. Sign and date your finished quilt.

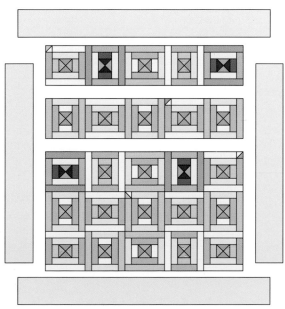

Quilt Assembly Diagram

Variable Jacob's Ladder

*T*he nine Jacob's Ladder pieced blocks are treated differently in this charmingly eccentric quilt. In some blocks, Sharon accentuated the small squares. In others they seem to be missing, but on further scrutiny you see them. Is the Ladder tipping? Oh dear, four blocks fell over, adding more intrigue to the composition, I hope. Hey, this is fun.

You can do a turn with any piece. Rotate the blocks for better blending and interest. It is especially important to try this with large floral blocks so they may blend into adjacent areas gracefully.

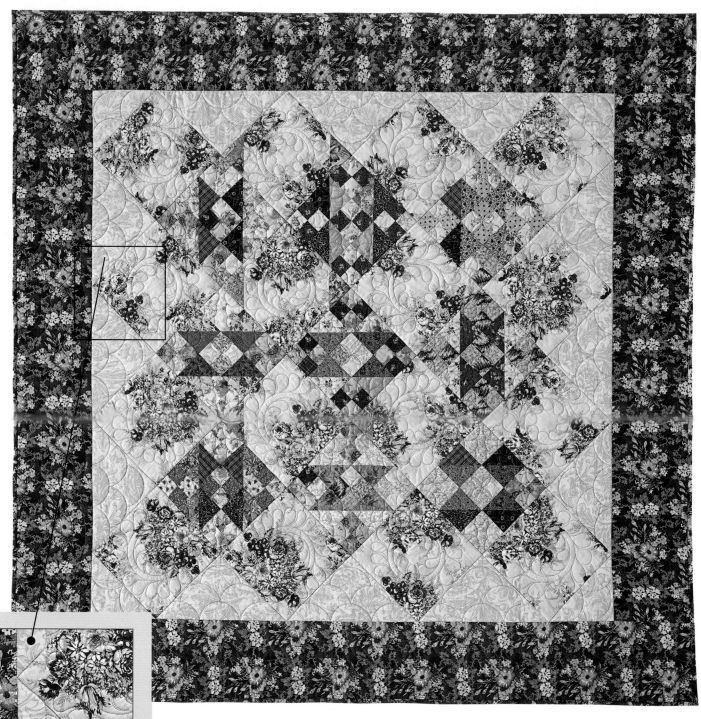

The neutral setting triangles allow your eyes to rest and make the block design appear to float on the surface.

Variable Jacob's Ladder

DESIGNED BY: **Sharon Yenter** QUILTED BY: **Sherry Rogers**
FINISHED SIZE: **66½" x 66½"** FINISHED BLOCK SIZE: **9" x 9"**

MATERIALS

Fabric requirements are based on 40" fabric width.

- 2¼ yds. all-over floral print (with red background) for border
- 1¼ yds. floral bouquet print (with beige background) for alternate blocks
- 1 yd. beige tone-on-tone print for side- and corner-setting triangles
- 8 or more assorted fat quarters for blocks— choose mostly light and medium prints with a few darks or brights for accent and sparkle
- ⅔ yd. for binding
- 4½ yds. for backing
- 75" x 75" batting

DIRECTIONS

Read these instructions thoroughly before starting. It's important to understand the whole process before you begin. Because the alternate blocks, setting triangles, and borders are so important to the overall design, you may want to cut them and place them in position on your design wall before making the Jacob's Ladder blocks. See *Basic Quiltmaking Techniques*, beginning on page 24, for general quiltmaking directions. All cutting measurements include ¼"-wide seam allowance.

Jacob's Ladder Blocks

9" Block

Cutting instructions are given for all 9 Jacob's Ladder blocks, but this is a scrappy treatment, and you may want to cut only a few patches at a time. It's fun to make fabric decisions as you go, and to see the overall quilt design grow on the design wall.

Cutting

From assorted fat quarters, cut:

- 36 squares, 3⅞" x 3⅞", for half-square triangle units
- 18 strips, 2" x 20+", for Fourpatch units

Assembly

1. Make 36 half-square triangle units, 4 for each block. Place 2 squares, 3⅞" x 3⅞", right sides together. With a pencil and acrylic ruler, draw a diagonal line from corner to corner. Measure ¼" on each side of diagonal line and draw stitching lines. Sew on each stitching line. Cut apart on diagonal line to make 2 half-square triangle units. Press seams toward darker fabric. Check completed unit to make sure it measures 3½" x 3½" (cut edge to cut edge).

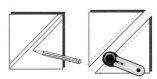

Make 36.

Fabric Selection Tips

Two large florals were chosen for the success of this quilt. One with a light ground, the other with a dark ground. Other colors chosen were keyed to go with one or both florals. Note the use of plaid in several blocks.

2. Make 45 Fourpatch units, 5 for each block. Using 18 strips, 2" x 20+", make 9 strip units. Press seams toward darker fabrics. Crosscut a total of 90 segments, each 2" wide.

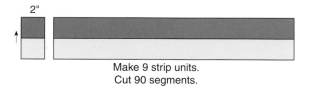

Make 9 strip units.
Cut 90 segments.

Arrange the segments in pairs and sew together to make Fourpatch units. Press seams to one side. Check completed units to make sure they measure 3½" x 3½" (cut edge to cut edge).

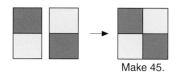

Make 45.

3. Working on a design wall, arrange the half-square triangle units and Fourpatch units into a total of 9 Jacob's Ladder blocks. Rearrange your component pieces until you are happy with the design. Sew half-square triangle units and Fourpatch units together in rows. Press seams toward Fourpatch units. Sew rows together to complete each block. Press seams to one side.

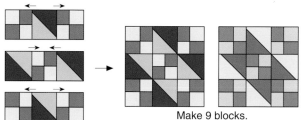

Make 9 blocks.
A variety of designs are possible,
depending on placement of lighter
and darker fabrics.

Setting Pieces
Cutting
From floral bouquet print, cut:
- 16 squares, 9½" x 9½", for alternate blocks

From assorted fat quarters, cut:
- 6 squares, 3½" x 3½", to be used as triangle accents on several alternate blocks (the squares will be trimmed after sewing)

From beige tone-on-tone print, cut:
- 3 squares, 14" x 14"; cut each square twice diagonally to make 12 side-setting triangles
- 2 squares, 7¼" x 7¼"; cut each square once diagonally to make 4 corner-setting triangles

Assembly
1. After arranging the 9 Jacob's Ladder blocks and alternate blocks on a design wall, decide which of the alternate blocks you want to accent. On the wrong side of the six 3½" accent squares, draw a diagonal line from corner to corner with a pencil and ruler.

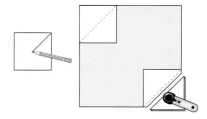

With right sides together, place a 3½" square in a corner (or corners) of the selected alternate blocks. Stitch on the pencil lines, then trim away the excess at each corner, leaving a ¼"-wide seam allowance. Press seams toward corner triangles.

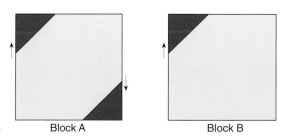

Block A   Block B

Examples of alternate blocks with triangle accents.
Sharon used 2 of Block A, and 2 of Block B in her quilt.

2. Join Jacob's Ladder blocks, alternate blocks, and side- and corner-setting triangles in diagonal rows as shown in the Quilt Assembly Diagram at right. Sew rows together.

Border

Cutting

From all-over floral print, cut:
- 4 strips the length of the fabric x 8" wide (Strips are cut longer than necessary and will be trimmed to size later.)

Assembly

1. Measure length of quilt through center. Trim 2 of the border strips to this measurement, and sew to sides of quilt top. Press seams toward border.
2. Measure width of quilt, including borders just added, through center. Trim remaining border strips to this measurement, and sew to top and bottom of quilt. Press seams toward border.

Finishing

1. Cut the backing fabric into two equal lengths and sew long edges together. Press seam open. Trim backing to 75" x 75".
2. Plan and mark quilting design as desired.
3. Layer quilt top, batting, and backing. Baste layers together.
4. Quilt by hand or machine.
5. Trim the batting and backing even with the quilt top edges.
6. Make and apply binding. From binding fabric, cut enough strips (each 2½" wide) either across the width of fabric, or across the bias, to make 281" of continuous binding. Bind the quilt edges.
7. Add a hanging sleeve if desired. Sign and date your finished quilt.

Quilt Assembly Diagram

Tipped Star

$\mathcal{T}$his quilt contains traditional stars
in a contemporary tipped set. The fabrics are reproductions from
the 1800s. Marsha bordered the quilt with a pieced strip of
random-length rectangles that repeat the fabrics in the interior
of the quilt. The use of seaweed and toile fabrics add interest
and make this a quilt that is fun to study, but exerts a feeling of
calm because of the mostly monochromatic colorway. Always
consider using interesting fabrics with different designs and scale
to elevate a quilt out of the ordinary.

The use of spaced, soft pink roses against the navy blue background changes this quilt from ordinary to elegant. Notice how the border fabrics are repeated in the interior of the quilt so your eyes are drawn in.

Tipped Star

DESIGNED BY: **Marsha McCloskey**   QUILTED BY: **Sherry Rogers**
FINISHED SIZE: **50½" x 60½"**   FINISHED BLOCK SIZE: **9" x 9"**

MATERIALS

Fabric requirements are based on 40" fabric width.

- 1½ yds. blue floral print for Sawtooth Stars, setting pieces, and outer border
- 4 or more assorted blue fat quarters for Sawtooth Stars, and outer border
- 1½ yds. blue toile for background of 8 Sawtooth Star blocks, and middle border
- ⅜ yd. medium-scale blue print for background of 4 Sawtooth Star blocks
- 1⅜ yds. floral stripe for inner border
- ⅝ yd. for binding
- 4¼ yds. for backing (if using lengthwise seam) OR 3½ yds. (if using widthwise seam)
- 59" x 69" batting

DIRECTIONS

Read these instructions thoroughly before starting. It's important to understand the whole process before you begin. Because the setting pieces, inner border, and middle border are so important to the overall design, you may want to cut them and place them in position on your design wall before making the Sawtooth Star blocks. See *Basic Quiltmaking Techniques*, beginning on page 24, for general quiltmaking directions. All cutting measurements include ¼"-wide seam allowance.

Sawtooth Star Blocks

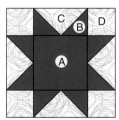

9" Block

Cutting

Only two fabrics are used in each Sawtooth Star block. In each block, your A and B pieces will be from one blue print, and your C and D pieces will be from one background print. It may be helpful to arrange your A, B, C, and D pieces on your design wall before sewing.

From blue floral print, cut:
- 6 squares, 5" x 5", for Squares A (1 for each of 6 blocks)
- 24 squares, 3⅛" x 3⅛"; cut each square once diagonally to make 48 Triangles B (8 for each of 6 blocks)

From assorted blue fat quarters, cut:
- 6 squares, 5" x 5", for Squares A (1 for each of 6 blocks)
- 24 squares, 3⅛" x 3⅛"; cut each square once diagonally to make 48 Triangles B (8 for each of 6 blocks)

From blue toile, cut:

(It's important to cut the blue toile pieces in the order given. Cut border pieces first, and set aside. From remaining fabric, cut squares for block piecing.)
- 4 strips the length of the fabric x 4½" wide, for middle border (Strips are cut slightly longer than necessary and will be trimmed to size later.)
- 8 squares, 5¾" x 5¾"; cut each square twice diagonally to make 32 Triangles C (4 for each of 8 blocks)
- 32 squares, 2¾" x 2¾", for Squares D (4 for each of 8 blocks)

Fabric Selection Tips

Dark monochromatic fabrics are pieced randomly to border the quilt. Add soft, contrasting inner borders to "quiet" the design.

From medium-scale blue print, cut:
- 4 squares, 5¾" x 5¾"; cut each square twice diagonally to make 16 Triangles C (4 for each of 4 blocks)
- 16 squares, 2¾" x 2¾", for Squares D (4 for each of 4 blocks)

Assembly

1. For each Sawtooth Star block you will need 1 Square A and 8 Triangles B of a blue print; and 4 Triangles C and 4 Squares D of a background print.

2. After determining fabric placement for each block, sew together 2 Triangles B and 1 Triangle C. Press seams toward Triangles B. Make 4 Triangle units for each block.

Make 4 for each block.
(48 total.)

3. Using Triangle units, Square A, and Squares D, assemble block rows as shown. Press seams toward squares. Join rows together. Press seams to one side. Repeat to make 12 Sawtooth Star blocks.

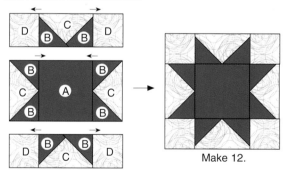

Make 12.

Setting Pieces
Cutting

From blue floral print, cut:
- 14 rectangles, 5" x 9½"; these will be used to make side-setting triangles
- 6 squares, 5" x 5", for setting squares

Assembly

1. Sew setting rectangles and squares to Sawtooth Star blocks as shown. Please note that, in the diagram, red lines indicate partial seams. Start and stop seams as red lines show. These partial seams will be finished in the next two steps.

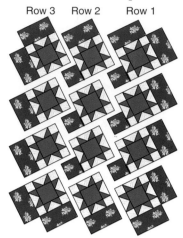

Row 3 Row 2 Row 1

2. Join Row 1 segments together. Press seams to one side. Following numbered sequence, join individual Row 2 segments to Row 1. At this point, you'll be finishing some of the partial seams. Press seams to one side.

Row 2 Row 1

3. Using the same technique as in Step 2, join Row 3 segments individually to Row 2. Press seams to one side.

Row 3

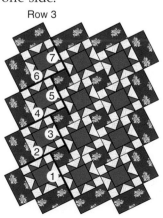

4. Square up and trim the edges of your quilt top, making sure to leave a ¼" seam allowance.

Borders
Cutting

From floral stripe, cut:
- 4 strips the length of the fabric x 2½" wide, for inner border (Strips are cut longer than necessary and will be trimmed to size later.)

From leftover blue floral print and assorted blue fat quarters, cut:
- 12 or more strips, 3½" wide x random lengths, for outer border

Inner Border Assembly

1. Measure length of the quilt through center. Trim 2 of the 2½"-wide floral stripe border strips to size, and sew to sides of quilt top. Press seams toward border.
2. Measure width of quilt, including borders just added, through center. Trim remaining 2½"-wide floral stripe border strips to size, and sew to top and bottom of quilt. Press seams toward border.

Middle Border Assembly

1. Using the 4½"-wide blue toile strips set aside earlier, and following general instructions for inner border assembly (above), add the middle border. Sew side borders first, then top and bottom.

Outer Border Assembly

1. Sew 3½"-wide, random-length blue print pieces together, end-to-end, to make 2 outer border strips at least 53" long, and 2 outer border strips at least 63" long.
2. Measure length of quilt through center. Trim 2 of the pieced border strips to size, and sew to sides of quilt top. Press seams toward middle border.
3. Measure width of quilt, including borders just added, through center. Trim remaining pieced border strips to size, and sew to top and bottom of quilt. Press seams toward middle border.

Finishing

1. Cut the backing fabric into two equal lengths and sew long edges together. Press seam open. Trim backing to 59" x 69".
2. Plan and mark quilting design as desired.
3. Layer quilt top, batting, and backing. Baste layers together.
4. Quilt by hand or machine.
5. Trim the batting and backing even with the quilt top edges.
6. Make and apply binding. From binding fabric, cut enough strips (each 2½"-wide) either across the width of fabric, or across the bias, to make 240" of continuous binding. Bind the quilt edges.
7. Add a hanging sleeve if desired. Sign and date your finished quilt.

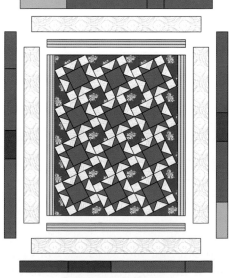

Quilt Assembly Diagram

Variable Ninepatch

*T*he ninepatch is a popular traditional pattern, but this one has twists. The alternate blocks contain a large floral, cut randomly, that sometimes blends into the pieced blocks making them almost disappear. The fourpatch blocks within the large ninepatch blocks create a dark chain in parts of the surface but then stop unexpectedly. We call this "breaking the pattern." Sharon (always the troublemaker!) disrupted the unity of the fourpatches and turned them into blending onepatches. Perhaps because onepatches are easier to sew? To chain or not to chain—that is your design dilemma. Accent your chains vertically, or horizontally, or both to make the quilt your own.

Small squares are stitched and appliquéd to the inset triangles to create an interesting design around the quilt interior. This is an easy technique that adds another element to the quilt.

Variable Ninepatch

DESIGNED BY: **Sharon Yenter**   QUILTED BY: **Sherry Rogers**
FINISHED SIZE: **70" x 70"**   FINISHED BLOCK SIZE: **9" x 9"**

MATERIALS

Fabric requirements are based on 40" fabric width, unless otherwise indicated.

- 1¼ yds. floral bouquet print (with pale yellow background) for alternate blocks
- 4¼ yds. blue toile for side- and corner-setting triangles, and border (Instructions are written for 40"-wide fabric. The sample uses 58"-wide decorator fabric. If using 58"-wide fabric, adjust fabric requirement to 3¼ yds. of blue toile.)
- 8 or more assorted fat quarters for blocks— include 2 medium-to-dark blues, 2 medium-to-dark roses or reds, and assorted light-to-medium large-scale prints that blend with the floral bouquet print
- ¼ yd. yellow print to use as accent for side-setting triangles
- ⅔ yd. for binding
- 4⅔ yds. for backing
- 78" x 78" batting

DIRECTIONS

Read these instructions thoroughly before starting. It's important to understand the whole process before you begin. Because the alternate blocks, setting triangles, and borders are so important to the overall design, you may want to cut them and place them in position on your design wall before making the Ninepatch blocks. See *Basic Quiltmaking Techniques*, beginning on page 24, for general quiltmaking directions. All cutting measurements include ¼"-wide seam allowance.

Ninepatch Blocks

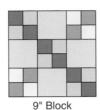

9" Block

Cutting instructions are given for all 9 Ninepatch blocks, but this is a scrappy treatment, and you may want to cut only a few patches at a time. It's fun to make fabric decisions as you go, and to see the overall quilt design grow on the design wall.

Cutting

From assorted fat quarters, cut:

- 50 squares, 3½" x 3½", for blocks
- 14 strips, 2" x 20+", for Fourpatch units (Cut additional strips for more variety.)

Assembly

1. Using 14 strips, 2" x 20+", make 7 strip units. Press seams toward darker fabrics. Crosscut a total of 62 segments, each 2" wide. (Make more if desired.)

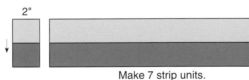

2"

Make 7 strip units.
Cut 62 segments.

Fabric Selection Tips

Choose a large toile for the oversize borders on this piece. Consider the width of the fabric in your plans as you probably don't want your figures laying down. This means the top and bottom must be cut crosswise and the sides lengthwise. In smaller-patterned, figured toiles this is usually unnecessary.

Arrange the segments in pairs and sew together to make 31 Fourpatch units. (Again, make more if desired.) Press seams to one side. Check completed units to make sure they measure 3½" x 3½" (cut edge to cut edge).

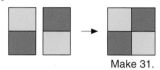

Make 31.

2. Working on a design wall, arrange 50 squares, 3½" x 3½", and 31 Fourpatch units into a total of 9 Ninepatch blocks. (If desired, you can use more Fourpatch units and fewer 3½" squares in your blocks.) Rearrange your component pieces until you are happy with the design.

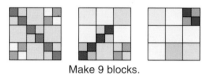

Make 9 blocks.
Place Fourpatch and Onepatch units as desired.
The examples show several arrangements used in Sharon's quilt.

3. Sew 3½" squares and Fourpatch units together in rows. Press for opposing seams. Sew rows together to complete each block. Press seams to one side.

Setting Pieces and Border
Cutting

From yellow print, cut:
- 12 squares, 3½" x 3½", to be appliquéd to side-setting triangles

From floral bouquet print, cut:
- 16 squares, 9½" x 9½", for alternate blocks

From blue toile, cut:
Note: *The top and bottom borders are cut across the width of the fabric to keep the direction of the design consistent. Unless fabric is 54" or wider, you will need to piece top and bottom borders to get the correct width.*

First, cut your blue toile yardage into two pieces: cut across the width of the fabric, making a 2½ yds. x 40" piece, and a 1¼ yds. x 40" piece.

Using 1¼ yds. piece of blue toile, cut:
- 3 strips across the width of the fabric, 10" x 40", for top and bottom borders (Plan your cuts so that the design will align from strip to strip. Yardage is generous to allow for matching design.)

Using 2½ yds. piece of blue toile, cut:
- 2 strips the length of the fabric x 10" wide, for side borders (Strips are cut longer than necessary and will be trimmed to size later.)
- 3 squares, 14" x 14"; cut each square twice diagonally to make 12 side-setting triangles
- 2 squares, 7¼" x 7¼"; cut each square once diagonally to make 4 corner-setting triangles

Side-Setting Triangle Assembly
Sharon appliquéd yellow accent squares to her triangles because she didn't want to break up the design of the toile with piecing. Repeat steps 1 and 2 twelve times.

1. Using an acrylic ruler for placement, with right sides together, position one of the 3½" yellow accent squares three inches from the inside edge of a side-setting triangle as shown. Pin square in place. Sew with a ¼"-wide seam, stopping ¼" from the raw edge at the corner as shown. Backstitch to secure.

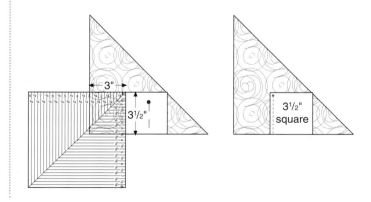

2. Fold the square over to fit in the corner of the side-setting triangle. Press the sewn seam. To finish the second side of the square, turn the raw edge under ¼"; then, using either a hand appliqué stitch, or a machine blind stitch, sew the side of the square to the setting triangle. Press. Trim away the side-setting triangle fabric that lies beneath the sewn-in square.

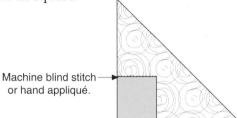

Machine blind stitch → or hand appliqué.

Quilt Top Assembly

1. Place the Ninepatch blocks, floral bouquet alternate squares, and triangles on the design wall. Move the parts around until the overall effect is pleasing. Look for interesting fabric and pattern combinations and opportunities for blending.
2. Following the Quilt Assembly Diagram on this page, join Ninepatch blocks, alternate squares, and setting triangles in diagonal rows as shown. Sew rows together.

Border Assembly

1. Arrange the 3 widthwise blue toile border strips so that the direction of the design is consistent. Sew the strips together to make one long strip. Press seams open.
2. Measure width of quilt through center. From the long strip, cut 2 border strips to match

this measurement. After making sure that the design orientation is correct, sew border strips to top and bottom of quilt top. Press seams toward border.
3. Place lengthwise blue toile border strips next to the sides of your quilt top, and adjust as needed for pleasing placement of the design. Measure length of quilt, including borders added in Step 2, through center. Trim the 2 border strips to this measurement, and join to sides of quilt. Press seams toward border.

Finishing

1. Cut the backing fabric into two equal lengths and sew long edges together. Press seam open. Trim backing to 78" x 78".
2. Plan and mark quilting design as desired.
3. Layer quilt top, batting, and backing. Baste layers together.
4. Quilt by hand or machine.
5. Trim the batting and backing even with the quilt top edges.
6. Make and apply binding. From binding fabric, cut enough strips (each 2½" wide) either across the width of fabric, or across the bias, to make 296" of continuous binding. Bind the quilt edges.
7. Add a hanging sleeve if desired. Sign and date your finished quilt.

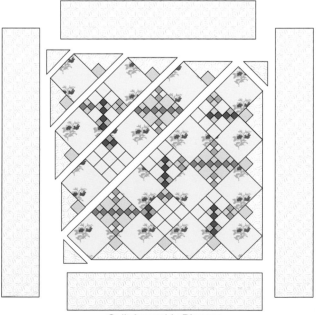

Quilt Assembly Diagram

Fourpatch Strippy

$\mathcal{S}$trippy patterns were very popular in the early 19th century. This is a variation using two easy blocks to create a vertical design. You create visual strips by careful placement of dark and light in the blocks, or you may create chains through the strips using contrasting fabrics. Notice how hard the beautiful sage toile is working to create a luxurious border. None of that tedious piecing for you! Save your creative genius for the center. Notice, also, how the side-setting border triangles are not all the same fabric. If you run out, use a substitute. Innovation, not perfection, is our goal.

You can create areas of blending by using low contrast fabrics as in the pink triangles, or create lines of higher contrast by using dark triangles.

Fourpatch Strippy

DESIGNED BY: **Sharon Yenter**   QUILTED BY: **Gretchen Engle**

FINISHED SIZE: **66½" x 75"**   FINISHED BLOCK SIZE: **6" x 6"**

MATERIALS

Fabric requirements are based on 40" fabric width.

- 2¼ yds. green toile for outer border
- 1¼ yds. floral bouquet print (with white background) for alternate blocks
- ½ yd. cream/green print for side- and corner-setting triangles
- ⅓ yd. pink toile for side-setting triangles
- 2 yds. pink/green floral stripe for inner border
- 10 or more assorted fat quarters for Double Fourpatch blocks and alternate blocks— choose mostly pinks and greens, with a few whites and yellows for sparkle
- ⅔ yd. for binding
- 5 yds. for backing
- 75" x 83" batting

DIRECTIONS

Read these instructions thoroughly before starting. It's important to understand the whole process before you begin. See *Basic Quiltmaking Techniques*, beginning on page 24, for general quiltmaking directions. All cutting measurements include ¼"-wide seam allowance.

Double Fourpatch Blocks

6" Block

Cutting instructions are given for all 20 Double Fourpatch blocks, but this is a scrappy

treatment, and you may want to cut only a few patches at a time. It's fun to make fabric decisions as you go, and to see the overall quilt design grow on the design wall.

Cutting

From assorted fat quarters, cut:

- 40 squares, 3⅞" x 3⅞", for half-square triangle units
- 16 or more* strips, 2" x 20+", for Fourpatch units
  *Cutting additional strips will allow for more variety when you begin strip-piecing your Fourpatch units.

Assembly

1. Make 40 half-square triangle units, 2 for each block. Place 2 squares, 3⅞" x 3⅞", right sides together. With a pencil and acrylic ruler, draw a diagonal line from corner to corner. Measure ¼" on each side of diagonal line and draw stitching lines. Sew on each stitching line. Cut apart on diagonal line to make 2 half-square triangle units. Press seams toward darker fabric. Check completed unit to make sure it measures 3½" x 3½" (cut edge to cut edge).

Make 40.

Fabric Selection Tips

Don't overlook patterned stripes for inner borders. In the early 1800s, this kind of stripe was cut up and sold in lengths specifically for quilts.

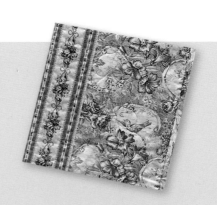

2. Make 40 Fourpatch units, 2 for each block. Using 16 strips, 2" x 20+", make 8 strip units. Press seams toward darker fabrics. Crosscut a total of 80 segments, each 2" wide.

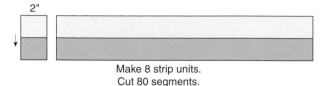

Make 8 strip units.
Cut 80 segments.

Arrange the segments in pairs and sew together to make Fourpatch units. Press seams to one side. Check completed units to make sure they measure 3½" x 3½" (cut edge to cut edge).

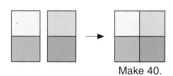

Make 40.

3. Working on a design wall, arrange the half-square triangle units and Fourpatch units into a total of 20 Double Fourpatch blocks. Rearrange your component pieces until you are happy with the design. Sew half-square triangle units and Fourpatch units together in pairs. Press seams toward half-square triangle units. Sew pairs together to complete each block. Press seams to one side.

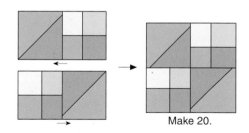

Make 20.

Setting Pieces
Cutting

From floral bouquet print, cut:
- 30 squares, 6½" x 6½", for alternate blocks

From assorted fat quarters, cut:
- 60 squares, 3½" x 3½", to be used as triangle accents on alternate blocks (the squares will be trimmed after sewing)

From cream/green print, cut:
- 4 squares, 9¾" x 9¾"; cut each square twice diagonally to make 16 side-setting triangles (3 extra)
- 2 squares, 5⅛" x 5⅛"; cut each square once diagonally to make 4 corner-setting triangles

From pink toile, cut:
- 2 squares, 9¾" x 9¾"; cut each square twice diagonally to make 8 side-setting triangles (3 extra)

Assembly

1. Make 30 alternate blocks. On the wrong side of 60 squares, 3½" x 3½", draw a diagonal line from corner to corner.

With right sides together, place two 3½" squares in opposite diagonal corners of a 6½" x 6½" floral bouquet square. Stitch on the pencil lines, then trim away the excess, leaving a ¼"-wide seam allowance. Press seams toward corner triangles. Repeat with the remaining 6½" squares.

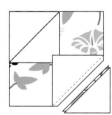 

Make 30.

2. Arrange the 20 Double Fourpatch blocks, 30 alternate blocks, and side- and corner-setting triangles on a design wall. Rearrange blocks until you are pleased with their placement.
3. Join blocks in diagonal rows as shown in the Quilt Assembly Diagram on page 87. Sew rows together.

Floral Stripe Border
Cutting
From pink/green floral stripe, cut:
- 4 strips the length of the fabric x 4⅝"* wide (Strips are cut longer than necessary and will be trimmed to size later.)
  *You might need to cut your border slightly wider or narrower depending on the design of your fabric.

Assembly
1. Measure length of quilt through center and add 11½". (If your floral stripe border strips are wider than designated above, add several more inches to allow for adjustments.) Trim 2 of the floral stripe border strips to this measurement, and sew to sides of quilt top; border strips will extend beyond top and bottom of quilt top. Press seams toward border.
2. Measure width of quilt, including borders just added, through center and add 3". (Again, if your floral stripe border strips are wider than designated above, add several more inches to allow for adjustments). Trim remaining floral stripe border strips to this measurement, and sew to top and bottom of quilt; strips will extend beyond edges of quilt. Press seams toward border.
3. Miter the border corners and trim excess fabric, leaving a ¼"-wide seam allowance. Press open.

Outer Border
Cutting
From green toile, cut:
- 4 strips the length of the fabric x 8" wide (Strips are cut longer than necessary and will be trimmed to size later.)

Assembly
1. Measure length of quilt through center. Trim 2 of the green toile border strips to this measurement, and sew to sides of quilt top. Press seams toward border.

2. Measure width of quilt, including borders just added, through center. Trim remaining green toile border strips to this measurement, and sew to top and bottom of quilt. Press seams toward border.

Finishing
1. Cut the backing fabric into two equal lengths and sew long edges together. Press seam open. Trim backing to 75" x 83".
2. Plan and mark quilting design as desired.
3. Layer quilt top, batting, and backing. Baste layers together.
4. Quilt by hand or machine.
5. Trim the batting and backing even with the quilt top edges.
6. Make and apply binding. From binding fabric, cut enough strips (each 2½" wide) either across the width of fabric, or across the bias, to make 300" of continuous binding. Bind the quilt edges.
7. Add a hanging sleeve if desired. Sign and date your finished quilt.

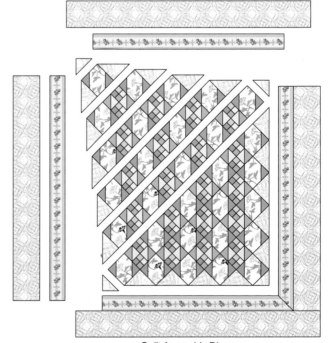

Quilt Assembly Diagram

Pinwheel Delight

*T*he Pinwheel pattern is traditionally constructed with very high contrast fabrics so that the design is accentuated. Barbara worked with a blending technique in each block. Her completed blocks form a soft, pleasing contrast against the neutral ground. The side-setting triangles stop the design with the use of several rich brown fabrics, very much in the style of an early 1800s quilt. Areas of light and dark blocks are seemingly placed randomly across the top although much thought was given to the composition. This quilt is more structured than some others in the book, but many traditional patterns could be set this way, opening up a whole new area of challenge.

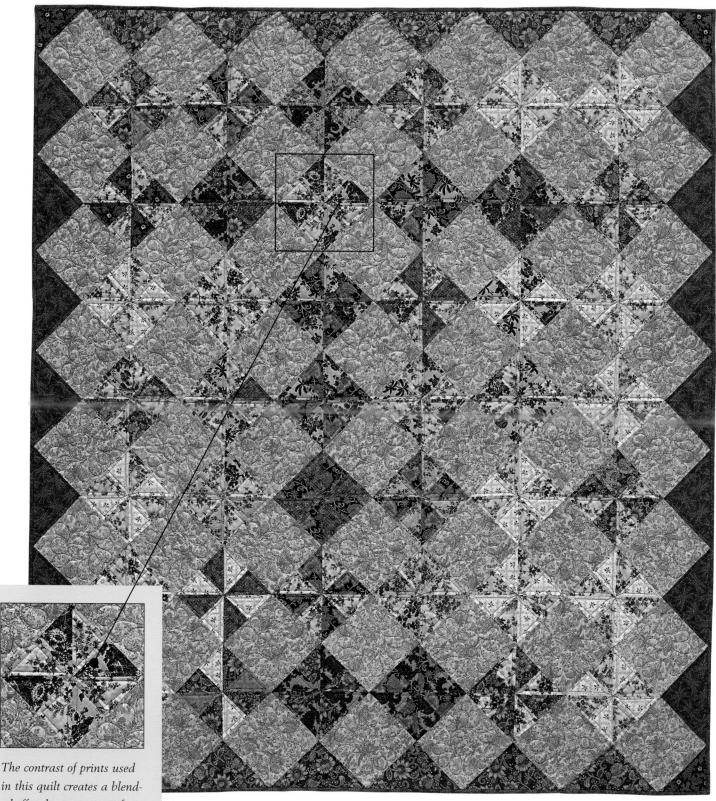

The contrast of prints used in this quilt creates a blended effect because a motif color in one fabric is picked up in another, allowing a unique combination.

Pinwheel Delight

DESIGNED BY: **Barbara Vose**   **QUILTED BY:** **Sherry Rogers**

FINISHED SIZE: 59½" x 68½"   **FINISHED BLOCK SIZE: 6" x 6"**

MATERIALS

Fabric requirements are based on 40" fabric width.

- 2⅓ yds. large-scale, light-value print for alternate blocks
- 1 yd. total of 3 or more medium/dark-value prints for side- and corner-setting triangles
- 9 or more assorted fat quarters for Pinwheel blocks
- ¾ yd. for binding
- 4½ yds. for backing (if using lengthwise seam) OR 4 yds. (if using widthwise seam)
- 68" x 77" batting

Tea-dyeing

You may discover fabrics in your collection that are too light. The old trick of tea-dyeing can work well here. You can achieve light or medium variations depending on the length of time you leave the fabric in the tea mixture.

1. Wash fabric using warm water and detergent.
2. Place 6 tea bags plus 2 teaspoons alum (used to set the color, it is available in drug stores) in a large glass bowl.
3. Bring 4 cups of water to a boil and pour into bowl. Stir with wooden spoon or chop sticks.
4. Cover bowl and allow tea to steep for 10 minutes. Remove tea bags.
5. Wet fabric completely and immerse it in tea solution in bowl.
6. Stir occasionally and check color every 10 minutes. You can get variations in color by dyeing multiple designs and removing some sooner than others. Your fabric will be much lighter dry than it appears when wet.
7. Remove when you are pleased with the color. Wash in warm, soapy water; rinse well, and hang to dry.

Another option instead of tea is Rit® dye. Ecru #18 and Taupe #34 are good choices for light to medium beige shades. Follow directions on the package and spend some time testing fabric scraps to get the color you want. Remember, a regular black tea such as Lipton® will have a redder tint as opposed to the more neutral Rit® dye shades.

DIRECTIONS

Read these instructions thoroughly before starting. It's important to understand the whole process before you begin. You may want to cut alternate blocks and setting triangles before making the Pinwheel blocks. See *Basic Quiltmaking Techniques*, beginning on page 24, for general quiltmaking directions. All cutting measurements include ¼"-wide seam allowance.

Fabric Selection Tips

Medium and small spaced florals and motifs are used to blend each block. Low to medium contrast is used to give a mellow, soft appearance.

Tip: Piecing Pinwheels

Here's a little trick for making the eight triangle points in the center of the Pinwheel block come together accurately.

1. Following assembly instructions, make 4 half-square triangle units.
2. Matching diagonal, opposing seams, chain piece 2 halves of the pinwheel. Make sure the triangles meet exactly at the ¼" seam line.

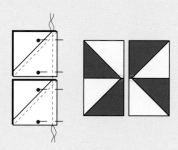

3. Press seams toward the darker fabric.
4. With the right sides together, use a positioning pin to match the points of the triangles at the center seams. Opposing vertical and diagonal seams will "nest." Pin as shown. Stitch center seam through the **X**. Press center seam open.

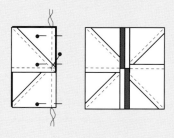

Pinwheel Blocks

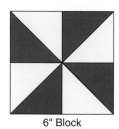

6" Block

Cutting instructions are given for all 42 Pinwheel blocks, but this is a scrappy treatment, and you may want to cut only a few patches at a time. It's fun to make fabric decisions as you go, and to see the overall quilt design grow on the design wall.

Cutting

From assorted fat quarters, cut:
- 168 squares, 3⅞" x 3⅞", to make half-square triangle units for Pinwheel blocks (4 squares—using at least 2 different prints—for each block)

Assembly

1. Make 168 half-square triangle units, 4 for each block. Place 2 squares, 3⅞" x 3⅞", right sides together. With a pencil and acrylic ruler, draw a diagonal line from corner to corner. Measure ¼" on each side of diagonal line and draw stitching lines. Sew on each stitching line. Cut apart on diagonal line to make 2 half-square triangle units. Press seams toward darker fabric. Check completed unit to make sure it measures 3½" x 3½" (cut edge to cut edge).

Make 168.

2. Sew 4 half-square triangle units together to make each Pinwheel block. (See Tip box for piecing and pressing hints.)

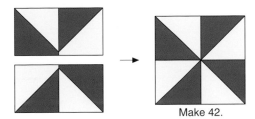

Make 42.

Setting Pieces

Cutting

From large-scale, light-value print, cut:
- 56 squares, 6½" x 6½", for alternate blocks

From medium/dark-value prints, cut:
- 7 squares, 9¾" x 9¾"; cut each square twice diagonally to make 28 side-setting triangles (2 extra)
- 2 squares, 5⅛" x 5⅛", cut each square once diagonally to make 4 corner-setting triangles

Assembly

1. Arrange Pinwheel blocks, alternate blocks, and side- and corner-setting triangles on the design wall. When you are pleased with the arrangement, join the pieces in diagonal rows as shown in the Quilt Assembly Diagram at right. Press seams toward alternate blocks.
2. Join rows together.

Finishing

1. Cut the backing fabric into two equal lengths and sew long edges together. Press seam open. Trim backing to 68" x 77".
2. Plan and mark quilting design as desired.
3. Layer quilt top, batting, and backing. Baste layers together.
4. Quilt by hand or machine.
5. Trim the batting and backing even with the quilt top edges.
6. Make and apply binding. From binding fabric, cut enough strips (each 2½" wide) either across the width of fabric, or across the bias, to make 276" of continuous binding. Bind the quilt edges.
7. Add a hanging sleeve if desired. Sign and date your finished quilt.

Quilt Assembly Diagram

Feathered Cross Medallion

*T*his frame or medallion quilt is very typical of the quilts produced in the mid- to late-1700s in America, and shows the influence of England on her colonists. The scrap triangle border gives you the opportunity to showcase unique reproduction fabrics or antique pieces you may have collected.

The inner borders are composed of blocks, strips, and pieces that begin and end randomly. The pieced inner borders have a total finished width of 6", and you may divide this measurement however you like. Notice the blending of florals in the lower area of the quilt. If you run out of one fabric, stitch in another…you'll be working in the spirit and tradition of many quilters in the early years of the United States.

Elegant, large, spaced floral blocks surround the Feathered Cross and make it appear to float. The color tone of the roses emphasizes the background color of the center square for unity.

Feathered Cross Medallion

DESIGNED BY: **Sharon Yenter**   QUILTED BY: **Gretchen Engle**

FINISHED SIZE: **48½" x 48½"**   FINISHED CENTER BLOCK SIZE: **18" x 18"**

MATERIALS

Fabric requirements are based on 40" fabric width.

- ¼ yd. each of 3 focal prints for center Feathered Cross block and outer border
- 14 or more assorted fat quarters for center Feathered Cross block, first border, and outer border
- ½ yd. all-over floral print for second border
- ½ yd. for binding
- 3½ yds. for backing
- 57" x 57" batting

DIRECTIONS

Read these instructions thoroughly before starting. See *Basic Quiltmaking Techniques,* beginning on page 24, for general quiltmaking directions. All cutting measurements include ¼"-wide seam allowance.

Feathered Cross Block

18" Block

Cutting

From focal prints, cut:

- 1 square, 6½" x 6½", for block center
- 4 squares, 6½" x 6½", for block corners

From assorted fat quarters, cut:

- 4 rectangles, 3½" x 6½", for block side-units

- 16 light squares, 2⅜" x 2⅜", for half-square triangles in block side-units
- 16 dark squares, 2⅜" x 2⅜", for half-square triangles in block side-units

Assembly

1. Make 32 half-square triangle units. Place 1 light square and 1 dark square, each 2⅜" x 2⅜", right sides together. With a pencil and acrylic ruler, draw a diagonal line from corner to corner. Measure ¼" on each side of diagonal line and draw stitching lines. Sew on each stitching line. Cut apart on diagonal line to make 2 half-square triangle units. Press seams toward darker fabrics. Check completed unit to make sure it measures 2" x 2" (cut edge to cut edge).

Make 32.

2. Sew 4 half-square triangle units together as shown. Press seams open. Make 4 of Triangle Row A, and 4 of Triangle Row B, making sure that orientation of triangles is correct in each row.

Triangle Row A
Make 4.

Triangle Row B
Make 4.

Fabric Selection Tips

The single fabric inner border consists of a reproduction fabric that was too bright and busy for the quilt, but had a lovely flow. Sharon reversed the cloth and used the "wrong" side. Remember this trick when searching for a soft, faded look to blend fabrics.

3. Make 4 side units. Sew a Triangle Row A and a Triangle Row B to each side of a 3½" x 6½" rectangle. Press seams toward rectangle.

Make 4.

4. Arrange the pieced side units, 6½" x 6½" center square, and 6½" x 6½" corner squares together in rows. Sew each row; press seams toward squares. Join rows together to finish block. Press seams to one side. Block should measure 18½" x 18½", edge to edge.

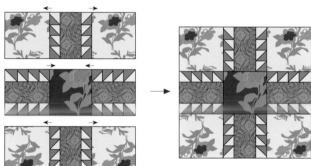

First Border
Cutting and Assembly

1. The innermost border is made up of many component pieces, including strips, squares, and small half-square triangle units. In designing your own border, you might start by cutting—from your fat quarters—an assortment of 2" strips, 3½" strips, and 2" x 2"

squares. If desired, make a batch of small half-square triangle units (piece as instructed in Feathered Cross Block Assembly, Step 1). Try strip-piecing Fourpatch or Ninepatch units. Using a design wall, arrange these components around your center block. Play with the arrangement, adding and subtracting pieces, until you are satisfied with the whole.

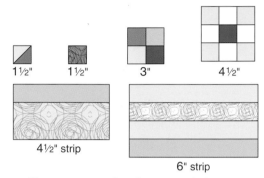

1½"   1½"   3"   4½"

4½" strip

6" strip

These are examples of component pieces which may be used in the first border. (Illustration measurements are finished sizes.)

2. Assemble each border. Keep in mind that the 2 side border strips should measure 6½" x 18½" with seam allowances. The top and bottom borders should measure 6½" x 30½". You can piece the borders to these exact lengths; or you can choose to make them longer, and cut them to size after they are assembled.

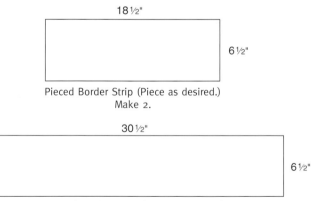

18½"

6½"

Pieced Border Strip (Piece as desired.)
Make 2.

30½"

6½"

Pieced Border Strip (Piece as desired.)
Make 2.

3. Sew the 18½"-long border strips to the sides of the Feathered Cross block as shown in the Quilt Assembly Diagram on this page. Press seams to one side.
4. Sew the 30½"-long border strips to the top and bottom of the Feathered Cross block. Press seams to one side.

Second Border
Cutting
From all-over floral print, cut:
- 2 strips, 3½" x 30½"
- 2 strips, 3½" x 36½"

Assembly
1. Sew 2 strips, 3½" x 30½", to sides of quilt. Press seams toward strips.
2. Sew 2 strips, 3½" x 36½", to top and bottom of quilt. Press seams toward strips.

Outer Border
Cutting
From focal prints, cut:
- 4 squares, 6½" x 6½", for corners

From assorted fat quarters, cut:
- 24 squares, 6⅞" x 6⅞", for half-square triangle units

Assembly
1. Make 24 half-square triangle units. Place 2 squares, 6⅞" x 6⅞", right sides together. With a pencil and acrylic ruler, draw a diagonal line from corner to corner. Measure ¼" on each side of diagonal line and draw stitching lines. Sew on each stitching line. Cut apart on diagonal line to make 2 half-square triangle units. Press seams toward darker fabrics.

Make 24.

2. Using triangle units and four 6½" x 6½" corner squares, sew border units as shown, making sure that orientation of triangles is

correct. Make 2 Border Strips A and 2 Border Strips B. Press seams to one side.

Border Strip A
Make 2.

Border Strip B
Make 2.

3. Sew Border Strips A to sides of quilt. Press seams toward second border.
4. Sew Border Strips B to top and bottom of quilt. Press seams toward second border.

Finishing

1. Cut the backing fabric into two equal lengths and sew long edges together. Press seam open. Trim backing to 57" x 57".
2. Plan and mark quilting design as desired.
3. Layer quilt top, batting, and backing. Baste layers together.
4. Quilt by hand or machine.
5. Trim the batting and backing even with the quilt top edges.
6. Make and apply binding. From binding fabric, cut enough strips (each 2½" wide) either across the width of fabric, or across the bias, to make 212" of continuous binding. Bind the quilt edges.
7. Add a hanging sleeve if desired. Sign and date your finished quilt.

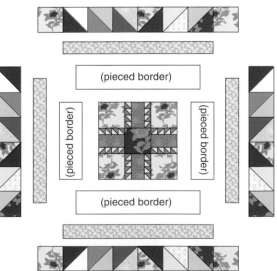

Quilt Assembly Diagram

Peppermint Fancy

*M*argy delights in high contrast for her
quilts and creates whimsical pieces that charm an audience. She is
something of a legend in quilting circles because a quilt she designed
and produced with children undergoing cancer treatment at Fred
Hutchinson Cancer Research Center, in Seattle, drew a winning bid
of $35,000.00. The bidding was animated among several CEOs, but
the quilt now resides in the corporate headquarters of Tully's Coffee
in Seattle. We suggested to Margy that she would enjoy the blended
technique and she proceeded as a "leap of faith." Peppermint Fancy
is the most contained quilt in the book, but it still follows many
design considerations for blended quilts, including: losing some
pattern by low contrast, flowing fabrics into each other, featuring a
large floral border, pulling color choices out of the border leaves and
Chrysanthemums, and using small- and medium-scale floral fabrics.
Margy made the choice to contrast the border and setting triangles,
but surprises us by keeping the sashing strips low-contrast enough
to blend and create a rich old-world charm.

Note the light, medium, and dark fabrics used for contrast. Shades of pinks to burgundy, and pale to dark greens, pick up motif colors in the light-background floral prints.

Peppermint Fancy

DESIGNED AND QUILTED BY: **Margy Duncan**
FINISHED SIZE: **61½" x 61½"** FINISHED BLOCK SIZE: **15" x 15"**

MATERIALS

Fabric requirements are based on 40" fabric width.

- 8 or more assorted fat quarters for blocks—include 3 or more pinks and reds, at least 2 greens, and at least 2 beiges or yellows
- ⅝ yd. green and gold print for sashing
- 1¼ yds. green print for side- and corner-setting triangles
- 2 yds. floral bouquet print for border
- ⅝ yd. for binding
- 4¼ yds. for backing
- 70" x 70" batting

DIRECTIONS

Read these instructions thoroughly before starting. It's important to understand the whole process before you begin. Because the setting pieces and border are so important to the overall design, you may want to cut them and place them in position on your design wall before making the Peppermint Fancy blocks. See *Basic Quiltmaking Techniques*, beginning on page 24, for general quiltmaking directions. All cutting measurements include ¼"-wide seam allowance.

Peppermint Fancy Blocks

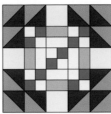

15" Block

Cutting instructions are given for all 5 Peppermint Fancy blocks, but this is a scrappy treatment, and you might want to cut only a few patches at a time. It's fun to make fabric decisions as you go, and to see the overall quilt design grow on the design wall.

Cutting

From assorted fat quarters, cut:

- 18 strips, 2" x 20+", for Fourpatch units and Bar units (use mostly green and beige/yellow prints)
- 60 squares, 3⅞" x 3⅞", for half-square triangle units (use red and pink prints)
- 20 squares, 3½" x 3½", (use beige/yellow prints)

Assembly

1. Make 25 Fourpatch units, 5 for each block. Using 10 strips, 2" x 20+", make 5 strip units. Press seams toward darker fabrics. Crosscut a total of 50 segments, each 2" wide.

Make 5 strip units.
Cut 50 segments.

Fabric Selection Tips

The use of a large-scale floral print with a light background adds a luxurious feel to this quilt and carries your eyes to the interior blocks. A dark background border would have given the piece a heavier look and allowed the five interior blocks to float. Not incorrect, but certainly different. Audition your borders with the completed top before making a final choice.

Arrange the segments in pairs and sew together to make Fourpatch units. Press seams to one side. Check completed units to make sure they measure 3½" x 3½" (cut edge to cut edge).

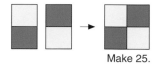

Make 25.

2. Make 20 Bar units, 4 for each block. Using 8 strips, 2" x 20+", make 4 strip units. Press seams toward darker fabrics. Crosscut a total of 20 Bar units, each 3½" wide.

3½"

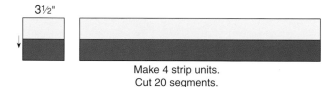

Make 4 strip units.
Cut 20 segments.

3. Make 60 half-square triangle units, 12 for each block. Place 2 squares, 3⅞" x 3⅞", right sides together. With a pencil and acrylic ruler, draw a diagonal line from corner to corner. Measure ¼" on each side of diagonal line and draw stitching lines. Sew on each stitching line. Cut apart on diagonal line to make 2 half-square triangle units. Press seams toward darker fabrics. Check completed units to make sure they measure 3½" x 3½" (cut edge to cut edge).

Make 60.

4. Make 5 Peppermint Fancy blocks. Join the Fourpatch units, Bar units, half-square triangle units, and 3½" squares together in rows. Press for opposing seams. Sew rows together. Press seams to one side.

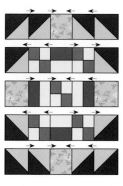

Make 5.
A variety of designs are possible, depending on placement of lighter and darker fabrics.

Sashing and Setting Triangles
Cutting
From green and gold print, cut:
- 3 strips; cut strips the width of the fabric, 2" x 40", for Sashing Strip C
- 2 pieces, 2" x 18½", for Sashing Strip B
- 8 pieces, 2" x 15½", for Sashing Strip A

From green print, cut:
- 1 square, 24⅝" x 24⅝"; cut square twice diagonally to make 4 side-setting triangles
- 2 squares, 13⅝" x 13⅝"; cut each square once diagonally to make 4 corner-setting triangles

Assembly

1. Sew the three 2" x 40" strips together end-to-end. Press seams open. From the long strip, cut 2 Sashing Strips C, each 2" x 51½".
2. Join the 2" x 15½" Sashing Strips A to blocks as shown in the Quilt Assembly Diagram on this page. Press seams toward sashing strips.
3. Sew the 2" x 18½" Sashing Strips B to one long side of the 2 remaining single blocks; and the 2" x 51½" Sashing Strips C to opposite sides of the 3-block row. Press seams toward sashing strips.
4. Sew side-setting triangles to blocks. Press seams toward triangles. Join rows together. Press seams to one side. Add corner-setting triangles. Press seams toward triangles.

Borders

Cutting

From floral bouquet print, cut:

- 4 strips the length of the fabric x 6½" wide (Strips are cut longer than necessary and will be trimmed to size later.)

Assembly

1. Measure length of quilt through center. Trim 2 floral bouquet strips to this measurement, and sew to sides of quilt top. Press seams toward border.
2. Measure width of quilt, including borders just added, through center. Trim remaining 2 floral bouquet strips to this measurement, and sew to top and bottom of quilt. Press seams toward border.

Finishing

1. Cut the backing fabric into two equal lengths and sew long edges together. Press seam open. Trim backing to 70" x 70".
2. Plan and mark quilting design as desired.
3. Layer quilt top, batting, and backing. Baste layers together.
4. Quilt by hand or machine.
5. Trim the batting and backing even with the quilt top edges.
6. Make and apply binding. From binding fabric, cut enough strips (each 2½" wide) either across the width of fabric, or across the bias, to make 264" of continuous binding. Bind the quilt edges.
7. Add a hanging sleeve if desired. Sign and date your finished quilt.

Quilt Assembly Diagram

Laura's Star

Laura, a well-known Pacific Northwest contemporary quiltmaker and author, with quilts in a museum and private collections, was excited to use new ideas and colorations to make her quilt work. She chose an easy star design with interior fourpatches. Both stars and fourpatch chains seem to appear and disappear. Working with lights, mediums, and darks, Laura created collages of exquisite fabric flowing across the rich surface. Large florals and paisleys blend to form secondary patterns. Soft peach tones are pulled from multi-color fabric motifs to create diagonal boxes of softness. This is a quilt you can study for a long time to discover design nuances.

*Laura uses areas of high
contrast to accentuate her
design. The use of viney
designs makes the light
sections flow into each other.
Notice how the dark areas
of paisley and florals blend
almost seamlessly.*

Laura's Star

DESIGNED AND QUILTED BY: **Laura Munson Reinstatler**
FINISHED SIZE: **65½" x 79½"** FINISHED BLOCK SIZE: **12" x 12"**

MATERIALS

Fabric requirements are based on 40" fabric width.

- 18 or more assorted fat quarters for blocks
- 2¼ yds. floral bouquet print for border
- ¾ yd. for binding
- 5¼ yds. for backing
- 74" x 88" batting

DIRECTIONS

Read these instructions thoroughly before starting. It's important to understand the whole process before you begin. See *Basic Quiltmaking Techniques*, beginning on page 24, for general quiltmaking directions. All cutting measurements include ¼"-wide seam allowance.

Star Blocks

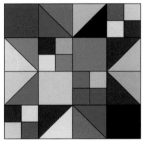

12" Star Block

Cutting instructions are given for all 20 Star blocks, but this is a scrappy treatment, and you may want to cut only a few patches at a time. It's fun to make fabric decisions as you go, and to see the overall quilt design grow on the design wall.

Cutting

From assorted fat quarters, cut:

- 32 strips, 2" x 20+", for Fourpatch units
- 160 squares, 3⅞" x 3⅞", for half-square triangle units
- 80 squares, 3½" x 3½"

Assembly

1. Make 80 Fourpatch units, 4 for each block. Using 32 strips, 2" x 20+", make 16 strip units. Press seams toward darker fabrics. Crosscut a total of 160 segments, each 2" wide.

2"

Make 16 strip units.
Cut 160 segments.

Arrange the segments in pairs and sew together to make Fourpatch units. Press seams to one side. Check completed units to make sure they measure 3½" x 3½" (cut edge to cut edge).

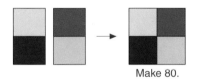

Make 80.

Fabric Selection Tips

The use of a large-scale floral print with a dark background creates an opulent border for this lush quilt, while the interior is light but mysterious and calls for examination. The many small-patterned fabrics read almost as solids and flow together to stop the clutter.

The dark border fabric was deliberately blended into the quilt blocks, making a graceful transition that leads your eyes to follow the dark designs.

2. Make 160 half-square triangle units, 8 for each block. Place 2 squares, 3⅞" x 3⅞", right sides together. With a pencil and acrylic ruler, draw a diagonal line from corner to corner. Measure ¼" on each side of diagonal line and draw stitching lines. Sew on each stitching line. Cut apart on diagonal line to make 2 half-square triangle units. Press seams toward darker fabrics. Check completed units to make sure they measure 3½" x 3½" (cut edge to cut edge).

Make 160.

3. Join the Fourpatch units, half-square triangle units, and 3½" squares together in rows. Press for opposing seams. Sew rows together. Press seams to one side.

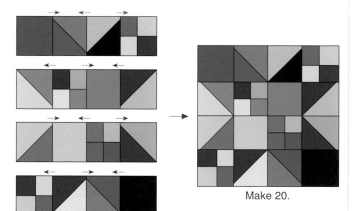

Make 20.

4. Sew Star blocks together in rows as shown in the Quilt Assembly Diagram on page 111. Press for opposing seams. Sew rows together. Press seams to one side.

Border
Cutting
From floral bouquet print, cut:
- 2 strips the length* of the fabric x 10" wide, for top and bottom borders
- 2 strips the length* of the fabric x 9" wide, for side borders
  *Strips are cut longer than necessary and will be trimmed to size later.

Assembly
1. Place the 9"-wide floral bouquet border strips next to the sides of your quilt top, and decide on the placement of the floral bouquets. Measure length of quilt through center. Trim the 2 floral bouquet strips to this measurement, and sew to sides of quilt top. Press seams toward outer border.

2. Measure width of quilt, including borders just added, through center. Arrange and trim the 10"-wide floral bouquet strips to this measurement, and sew to top and bottom of quilt. Press seams toward outer border.

Finishing

1. Cut the backing fabric into two equal lengths and sew long edges together. Press seam open. Trim backing to 74" x 88".
2. Plan and mark quilting design as desired.
3. Layer quilt top, batting, and backing. Baste layers together.
4. Quilt by hand or machine.
5. Trim the batting and backing even with the quilt top edges.
6. Make and apply binding. From binding fabric, cut enough strips (each 2½" wide) either across the width of fabric, or across the bias, to make 308" of continuous binding. Bind the quilt edges.
7. Add a hanging sleeve if desired. Sign and date your finished quilt.

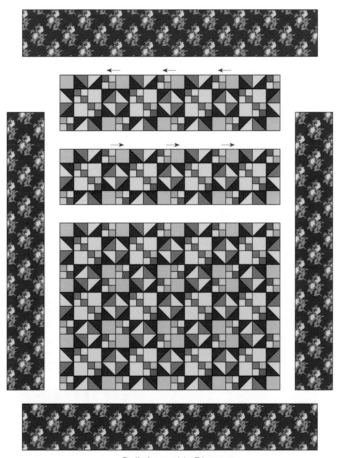

Quilt Assembly Diagram

Floribundus

$\mathcal{S}$elective cutting makes this quilt a show-stopper. Barbara planned each piece to blend and develop into a textured surface of elegance. Large and medium floral patterns with leafy areas, vines, and tendrils flow into each other and create a graceful cascade of color across the quilt. The borders are cut in strips to feature the area between the floral bouquets. This selective cutting may yield odd pieces of extra background fabric. You can often use these for smaller pieces in your quilt or save them for decorative pillows. Always cut your border lengths first before you cut any squares from the fabric.

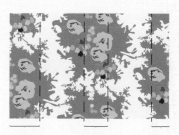

Scrap   Scrap   Scrap

Notice the nine squares of large red flowers placed as an accent in the center of the quilt. The placement adds sparkle and draws your eyes into the design.

Floribundus

DESIGNED BY: **Barbara Vose**   QUILTED BY: **Gem Taylor**

FINISHED SIZE: **39½" x 51½"**   FINISHED UNIT SIZE: **3" x 3"**

MATERIALS

Fabric requirements are based on 40" fabric width.

- 1⅓ yds.* floral bouquet print for border
- 1¼ yds. total of 3 or more floral prints for triangle units and 3½" squares
- 1 yd. total of 2 background prints for piecing (look for 1 light-value print, and 1 lighter-value print)
- ½ yd. for binding
- 3½ yds.** for backing
- 48" x 60" batting

*Yardage is generous to allow for selective placement of floral bouquet design.
**If you don't mind working with a smaller-than-usual margin of backing fabric in your "quilt sandwich," it's possible to get the backing out of one length (rather than two) of 44-45"-wide fabric. In that case, you'll need 1¾ yds. backing fabric.

DIRECTIONS

Read these instructions thoroughly before starting. It's important to understand the whole process before you begin. See *Basic Quiltmaking Techniques*, beginning on page 24, for general quiltmaking directions. All cutting measurements include ¼"-wide seam allowance.

Triangle Units

3" Unit   3" Unit

Cutting

From floral prints, cut:

- 29 squares, 4¼" x 4¼"
- 4 squares (2 squares each from 2 different prints), 3⅞" x 3⅞"; cut each square once diagonally to make 8 triangles

From light- and lighter-value background prints, cut:

- 29 squares, 4¼" x 4¼"

Assembly

1. Make 4 half-square triangle units for corners of quilt center design. For each, join 2 floral-print triangles. Press seams to one side.

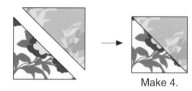

Make 4.

2. Make 58 half-square triangle units (these will be made into quarter-square triangle units in Step 3). With right sides together, arrange the 4¼" squares in pairs of a floral-print square and a background print. Working with one

Fabric Selection Tips

The soft, romantic look of this quilt can be achieved with just six or seven fabrics. Large, light peach florals, cut randomly, add texture and a subtle "lighting" of the center. Two flowing background prints, one slightly lighter than the other, create a blended floral design in the corners and borders.

pair of squares at a time, make a cut diagonally, corner to corner, yielding 2 pairs of triangles. Stitching the long side, sew each triangle pair together with ¼" seams. Press seams to one side. Check completed unit to make sure it measures 3⅞" x 3⅞" (cut edge to cut edge).

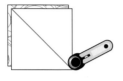

Make 58.

3. To make 58 quarter-square triangle units, match pairs of half-square triangle units, right sides together, nesting opposing seams. Cut squares diagonally and sew resulting triangle pairs together with ¼" seams. Press seams to one side. Check completed unit to make sure it measures 3½" x 3½" (cut edge to cut edge).

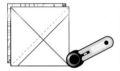

Make 58.

Alternate Squares
Cutting
From light- and lighter-value background prints, cut:
- 20 squares, 3½" x 3½"

From floral prints, cut:
- 43 squares, 3½" x 3½"; 35 for quilt center and 8 for border

Assembly

1. On a design wall, arrange the 3½" x 3½" squares, the half-square triangle units, and the quarter-square triangle units in the pattern shown. For a lit-from-within effect, place your lighter pieces near the center. When you are happy with the design, assemble the units into 13 rows as shown. Press seams toward squares.

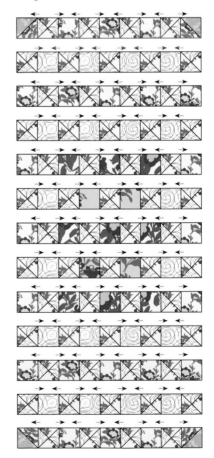

2. Sew the rows together. Press seams to one side.

Borders

Cutting

From floral bouquet print, cut:

- 2 strips,* 6½" x 21½"
- 2 strips,* 6½" x 33½"
- 8 squares, 3½" x 3½"
- 4 squares, 6½" x 6½"

*Before cutting border strips, determine whether you want selective placement of floral bouquet design in your border. Cut accordingly. (See page 112.)

Assembly

1. Make 8 two-square units. Join a 3½" floral-print square to a 3½" floral-bouquet-print square. Press seams to one side.

2. Make 2 long border strips as shown in the Quilt Assembly Diagram on this page. Sew a 2-square unit to each end of a 6½" x 33½" strip. Press seams toward strip. Sew long border strips to sides of quilt. Press seams toward border.

3. Make 2 short border strips. Join a 2-square unit to each end of a 6½" x 21½" strip. Press seams toward strip. Add a 6½" floral-bouquet-print square to each end of this strip. Press seams toward 2-square units. Sew border strips to top and bottom of quilt. Press seams toward border.

Finishing

1. Cut the backing fabric into two equal lengths and sew long edges together. Press seam open. Trim backing to 48" x 60".

2. Plan and mark quilting design as desired.

3. Layer quilt top, batting, and backing. Baste layers together.

4. Quilt by hand or machine.

5. Trim the batting and backing even with the quilt top edges.

6. Make and apply binding. From binding fabric, cut enough strips (each 2½" wide) either across the width of fabric, or across the bias, to make 200" of continuous binding. Bind the quilt edges.

7. Add a hanging sleeve if desired. Sign and date your finished quilt.

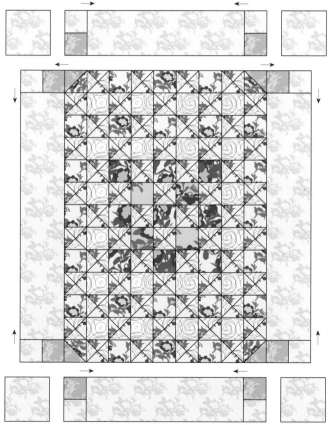

Quilt Assembly Diagram

Victoria's Garden

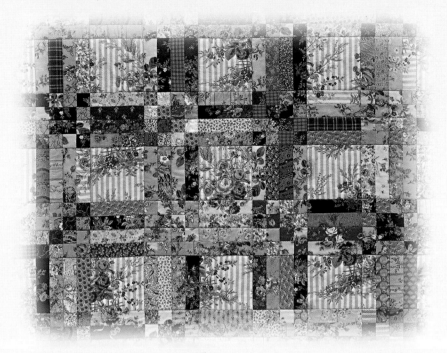

*I*f you want a certain portion of your

floral bouquet to appear regularly and evenly in all four borders,

you will need to plan the border carefully. Many blended quilts

are planned with uneven bouquet borders, but Vicki wanted hers

to repeat in a balanced manner. She purchased extra fabric so

she could work with the design. A graceful, floral curve is created

around the quilt when bouquets meet in the corners. To get this

effect, you may want to start with the border fabric and size your

quilt to this requirement, making it larger or smaller depending

on the floral pattern repeat. Or you may choose to use Vicki's

technique. From her leftover border fabric, she selected flowers,

added a quarter inch, cut and appliquéd them in the corners

to create sumptuous Victorian bouquets.

The pattern for this quilt originated with a 12" block design, but Vicki realized that it would be easier to blend fabrics if she divided the blocks into 6" finished squares.

Victoria's Garden

DESIGNED BY: **Victoria Hurst**   QUILTED BY: **Gretchen Engle**
FINISHED SIZE: **76½" x 88½"**   FINISHED BLOCK SIZE: **6" x 6"**

MATERIALS

Fabric requirements are based on 40" fabric width.

- 18 or more assorted fat quarters for Strippy blocks and 16-patch blocks
- 1½ yds.* floral bouquet print #1 for Onepatch blocks
- 3 yds.* floral bouquet print #2 for border
- ¾ yd. for binding
- 8½ yds.** for backing
- 85" x 97" batting

  *Yardage is generous to allow for selective placement of floral bouquet design.

  **If you don't mind working with a smaller-than-usual-margin of backing fabric in your "quilt sandwich," it's possible to get the backing out of two lengths (rather than three) of 44-45"-wide fabric. In that case, you'll need 5¾ yds. backing fabric.

DIRECTIONS

Read these instructions thoroughly before starting. It's important to understand the whole process before you begin. See *Basic Quiltmaking Techniques*, beginning on page 24, for general quiltmaking directions. All cutting measurements include ¼"-wide seam allowance.

Blocks

6" Blocks

Cutting instructions are given for twenty 16-patch blocks and 49 Strippy blocks, but this is a scrappy treatment, and you may want to cut only a few strips for strip-pieced units at a time. It's fun to make fabric decisions as you go, and to see the overall quilt design grow on the design wall.

Cutting

From assorted fat quarters, cut:

- 136 strips, 2" x 20+", for Strippy blocks and 16-patch blocks

From floral bouquet print #1, cut:

- 30 squares, 6½" x 6½", for Onepatch blocks

  Note: *Vicki cut her squares randomly without centering each floral design. After cutting, she looked through them and discarded those that didn't show a pleasing section of the design. Generous yardage allowed her to cut new squares to replace the unsatisfactory ones.*

Fabric Selection Tips

A floral stripe was chosen for background interest. See how the floral fabrics blend into each other and blur the construction lines. Dark rectangles are introduced into the interior of the quilt to "tie in" the wide, dark border. Notice how your eyes move around the quilt, studying the composition.

Assembly

1. Using 136 strips, 2" x 20+", make 68 strip units. Press seams toward darker fabrics. Crosscut a total of 240 segments, each 2" wide, and 120 segments, each 6½" wide. For good variety make sure that, from each strip unit, you cut segments of both widths (2" and 6½").

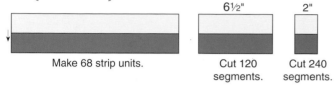

6½"   2"

Make 68 strip units.   Cut 120 segments.   Cut 240 segments.

Cutting Tip

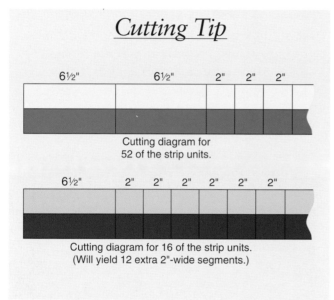

6½"   6½"   2"   2"   2"

Cutting diagram for 52 of the strip units.

6½"   2"   2"   2"   2"   2"   2"

Cutting diagram for 16 of the strip units.
(Will yield 12 extra 2"-wide segments.)

---

2. Fourpatch units: Arrange the 2"-wide segments in pairs and sew together to make 120 Fourpatch units. Press seams to one side. Check completed units to make sure they measure 3½" x 3½" (cut edge to cut edge). Set aside 4 Fourpatch units for corners.

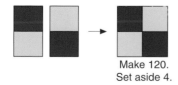

Make 120.
Set aside 4.

3. Double-Fourpatch units: Arrange 116 Fourpatch units in pairs and sew together to make 58 Double-Fourpatch units. Press seams to one side. Set aside 18.

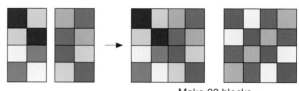

Make 58.
Set aside 18.

4. 16-patch blocks: Arrange 40 Double-Fourpatch units in pairs and sew together to make twenty 16-patch blocks. Press seams to one side.

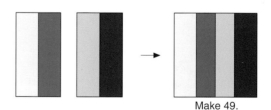

Make 20 blocks.
You can achieve different design effects by playing with the placement of lighter and darker fabrics.

5. Strippy blocks: Set aside 22 of the 6½"-wide strip-pieced segments. Arrange 98 remaining 6½"-wide segments in pairs and sew together to make 49 Strippy blocks.

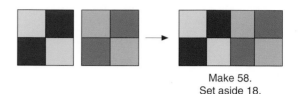

Make 49.

6. Following the Quilt Assembly Diagram on page 123, join the Fourpatch corner units, Double-Fourpatch units, 16-patch blocks, Strippy segments and blocks, and floral bouquet Onepatch blocks together in rows. Press for opposing seams. Sew rows together. Press seams to one side.

Border

Cutting

From floral bouquet print #2, cut:

- 4 strips the length of the fabric x 8½" wide (Strips are cut longer than necessary and will be trimmed to size later.)

Assembly

1. Measure width of quilt through center. Trim 2 floral bouquet print #2 strips to this measurement, and sew to top and bottom of quilt top. Press seams toward border.

2. Measure length of quilt, including borders just added, through center. Trim remaining 2 floral bouquet print #2 strips to this measurement, and sew to sides of quilt. Press seams toward border.

3. Vicki used the broderie perse technique to fill out the bouquets at the corners of her borders. From her leftover fabric, she cut selected flowers, adding a ¼" seam allowance all around. After pinning the flowers in place, she turned under the edges and appliquéd them in place. The result: beautifully blooming borders all the way around her quilt.

Broderie perse addition to complete flower

Finishing

1. Cut the backing fabric into three equal lengths (if using 5¾ yds. of backing fabric, cut into two equal lengths) and sew long edges together. Press seams open. Trim backing to 85" x 97".

2. Plan and mark quilting design as desired.

3. Layer quilt top, batting, and backing. Baste layers together.

4. Quilt by hand or machine.

5. Trim the batting and backing even with the quilt top edges.

6. Make and apply binding. From binding fabric, cut enough strips (each 2½" wide) either across the width of fabric, or across the bias, to make 348" of continuous binding. Bind the quilt edges.

7. Add a hanging sleeve if desired. Sign and date your finished quilt

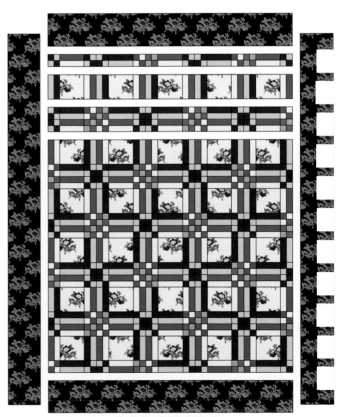

Quilt Assembly Diagram

Northwind

*T*he borders we have used on the blended quilts are easy but very effective. The toile borders in this quilt might tell a scenic story. They are combined with a lovely reproduction French stripe that might have existed in Josephine's court. Only the sides are edged with triangles. But notice the interruptions where the triangles are replaced by lovely strips of fabric. You have permission to stop anywhere…it's your choice! The fabrics in the inner border are inconsistent also; they are similar colors, but different prints. The ninepatch blocks are consistently spaced but they don't have to be. They could be different traditional pieced blocks or plain squares of fabric. Isn't this fun? Do what works for you. You will find that choosing and blending the fabrics are your most difficult decisions, but you will learn so much about color, design, and your preferences as you play with your choices.

Rotating blocks for blending or contrast can add exciting design elements to your composition. High contrast and low contrast blocks blend easily to form abstract elements.

Northwind

DESIGNED BY: **Marsha McCloskey** QUILTED BY: **Gem Taylor**
FINISHED SIZE: **77½" x 75½"** FINISHED BLOCK SIZE: **9" x 9"**

MATERIALS

Fabric requirements are based on 40" fabric width.

- 22 or more assorted fat quarters for Northwind blocks, Ninepatch border, and Sawtooth border — choose mostly medium-value prints, with a few lights and darks for accents and sparkle
- 1 yd. green toile for side- and corner-setting triangles
- 1⅞ yds. floral stripe for side borders
- 1 yd. brown toile for top and bottom borders
- ¾ yd. for binding
- 7½ yds.* for backing
- 86" x 84" batting
  *If you don't mind working with a smaller-than-usual-margin of backing fabric in your "quilt sandwich," it's possible to get the backing out of two lengths (rather than three) of 44-45"-wide fabric. In that case, you'll need 5 yds. backing fabric.

DIRECTIONS

Read these instructions thoroughly before starting. It's important to understand the whole process before you begin. See *Basic Quiltmaking Techniques*, beginning on page 24, for general quiltmaking directions. All cutting measurements include ¼"-wide seam allowance.

Northwind Blocks

9" Block

Cutting instructions are given for all 24 Northwind blocks, but this is a scrappy treatment, and you may want to cut only enough patches for one block at a time. The fun is in finding "blendy" fabric combinations for each block.

Cutting

From assorted fat quarters, cut:
- 24 squares, 6⅞" x 6⅞"; cut each square once diagonally to make 48 large triangles for Northwind blocks (2 triangles — using 2 different prints — for each block)
- 120 squares, 3⅞" x 3⅞"; cut each square once diagonally to make 240 small triangles for Northwind blocks (10 triangles — using at least 2 different prints — for each block)

Assembly

Instructions are for one block. Repeat 24 times.

1. Sew together 2 small triangles. Press seams toward darker fabric. Make 3 of these half-square triangle units.

Make 3.

2. Join 4 small triangles to half-square triangle units in rows as shown. Join rows together. Press seams to one side.

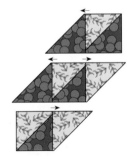

Fabric Selection Tips

French "look" reproductions are important to the vintage elegance of this quilt. Toiles, floral stripes, spaced and bouquet florals in medium and large sizes are cut to look random, but are planned to flow into each other. Study each block to understand the interaction of fabric and patterns.

3. Sew 2 large triangles to opposite sides of sewn unit. Press seams toward large triangles.

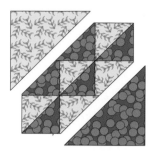

Setting Pieces
Cutting
From green toile, cut:
- 2 squares, 14" x 14"; cut each square twice diagonally to make 8 side-setting triangles
- 2 squares, 13⅝" x 13⅝"; cut each square once diagonally to make 4 corner-setting triangles

Assembly
1. After making sure the design orientation of the toile is correct (all the figures standing up), join blocks and side-setting triangles in diagonal rows as shown. Press seams to one side. Sew rows together.
2. Add corner-setting triangles to each corner. Press seams toward triangles.

Ninepatch Border

4½" Block

Cutting
From assorted fat quarters, cut:
- 7 strips (light value), 2" x 20+", for Ninepatch blocks
- 8 strips (medium value), 2" x 20+", for Ninepatch blocks
- 8 pieces, 5" x 13¼", for Ninepatch border (Rectangle A)
- 4 pieces, 5" x 17", for Ninepatch border (Rectangle B)

Assembly
1. Using 3 strips, 2" x 20+", of assorted light-value prints; and 6 strips, 2" x 20+", of assorted medium-value prints, make 3 of Strip Unit A. Press seams toward medium-value strips. Crosscut a total of 24 segments, each 2" wide.

Make 3 of Strip Unit A.
Cut 24 segments.

2. Using 4 strips, 2" x 20+", of assorted light-value prints; and 2 strips, 2" x 20+" of assorted medium-value prints, make 2 of Strip Unit B. Press seams toward medium-value strip. Crosscut a total of 12 segments, each 2" wide.

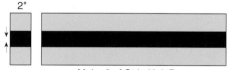

Make 2 of Strip Unit B.
Cut 12 segments.

3. Join the segments from steps 1 and 2 to make 12 Ninepatch blocks. Press seams to one side.

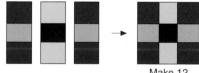

Make 12.

4. Join Ninepatch blocks, 5" x 13¼" Rectangles A, and 5" x 17" Rectangles B in border strips as shown.

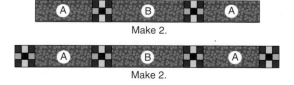

Make 2.

Make 2.

5. Sew the 2 shorter Ninepatch border strips to opposite sides of quilt as shown in Quilt Assembly Diagram on this page. Press seams to one side. Sew the 2 longer Ninepatch border strips to top and bottom of quilt. Press seams to one side.

Plain Border
Cutting
From floral stripe, cut:
- 2 strips, 6" x 60½", for side borders

From brown toile, cut:
- 4 strips, 8" x 40" (the width of the fabric), for top and bottom borders

Assembly
1. Sew the 6"-wide floral stripe border strips to opposite sides of quilt. Press seams toward side borders.
2. Join two 8"-wide brown toile border strips end-to-end, making sure the direction of the design is consistent. Repeat to make two long strips.
3. Measure width of quilt through center. From the toile strips, cut 2 border strips to match this measurement. After making sure the design orientation is correct, sew border strips to top and bottom of quilt top. Press seams toward border.

Sawtooth Border
Cutting
From assorted fat quarters, cut:
- 35-50 squares, 3⅞" x 3⅞"; cut each square once diagonally to make 70-100 small triangles for Sawtooth border
- 3 strips, 3½" x 20+", for Sawtooth border

Assembly
1. Sew together 2 small triangles. Press seams toward darker fabric. Make 35-50 of these Sawtooth units.

Make 35-50.

2. Sew the Sawtooth units in random rows as desired. Plan 2 border strips, using the Sawtooth rows and your 3½" x 20+" strips. Trim the 3½"-wide strips to size to fill the border between the Sawtooth rows. When sewn together, your Sawtooth border strips should measure 3½" x 75½".

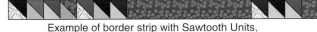

Example of border strip with Sawtooth Units, and random lengths of 3½"-wide fabric. Make 2 border strips, each 3½" x 75½".

3. Sew 2 Sawtooth border strips to opposite sides of quilt. Press seams toward plain border.

Finishing
1. Cut the backing fabric into three equal lengths (if using 5 yds. of backing fabric, cut into two equal lengths) and sew long edges together. Press seams open. Trim backing to 86" x 84".
2. Plan and mark quilting design as desired.
3. Layer quilt top, batting, and backing. Baste layers together.
4. Quilt by hand or machine.
5. Trim the batting and backing even with the quilt top edges.
6. Make and apply binding. From binding fabric, cut enough strips (each 2½" wide) either across the width of fabric, or across the bias, to make 324" of continuous binding. Bind the quilt edges.
7. Add a hanging sleeve if desired. Sign and date your finished quilt.

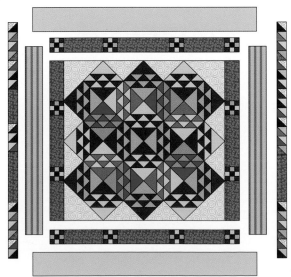

Quilt Assembly Diagram

Gaches Mansion

Many of the quilts in this book were photographed at the La Conner Quilt Museum in La Conner, Washington. The town, situated 70 miles north of Seattle, is located in a picturesque area in the shadow of majestic Mount Baker, and is known as the gateway to the San Juan Islands and the spectacular Northern Cascades highway.

The fertile fields of Skagit Valley welcome visitors from around the world when spring bursts forth with acres of tulips, daffodils, and iris at the annual Tulip Festival. Today, La Conner is listed on the National Register of Historic Places and is brimming with antique shops, galleries, restaurants, and bed and breakfasts.

The museum, one of only 10 quilt museums in the U.S.A., is housed in the Gaches Mansion, a beautiful and stately home built in 1891 by mercantile-owner and entrepreneur, George Gaches. Beginning as a private residence, the mansion, over the years, evolved into a hospital, returned to its status as a single-family home, and finally became the Castle Apartments before being gutted in a 1973 fire.

Mounting an effort to preserve their history, local citizens formed La Conner Landmarks and bought the badly damaged mansion. With the help of the Federal Historic Preservation and the Washington State Parks and Recreation Commission, they undertook a full restoration. In September 1997, the La Conner Quilt Museum took up residence at the mansion, with Rita Hupy as Director.

Quilters should allow themselves plenty of time at the Quilt Museum. Exploring the authentically-furnished first floor of the mansion is almost as much fun as viewing the quilt shows displayed on the second and third floors. There are five exhibits a year, representing contemporary and traditional quiltmaking from the United States and abroad. Some shows feature the work of a single quilter; other shows are drawn from historical and regional collections. All are worth a visit!

Hours: Wednesday through Saturday, 10-4; Sunday, 12-4. Open only weekends in December. Phone: (360) 466-4288.

Acknowledgements

A book project takes much talent and patience from many people to see it through. Thanks to Marsha McCloskey and Wendy Slotboom for their knowledge and sense of fun. Our friends at Sea-Hill Press, especially Barbara for her easy manner and exciting design ideas. The quilt designers and quilters did a wonderful job and were always willing to contribute more than asked for. This was a 110% team effort and so many people contributed.

Thanks to our staff at In The Beginning who are always supportive and generous. A special thanks to Jason Yenter and Trish Carey for help with the intense days of the photo shoot.

Our photographers Ken Wagner and Jay Dotson make their work look simple, but they are easy-going professionals whose expert decisions make our quilt photographs and settings look phenomenal.

Thanks also to Rita Hupy and her staff at the La Conner Quilt Museum. The mansion is a treasure and a magic place to work. Finally, I can't express enough thanks to my wonderful family who have seen me through 25 years at In The Beginning. Your love and support are the most important things in my life.

— *Sharon Yenter*

My personal thanks go to Sharon Yenter for involving me in the *Blended Quilts* project and prodding me to see and use prints in a new way. Also to Barb Vose and Wendy Slotboom for their continuing help and support. And to my family without whom, none of this would matter.

— *Marsha McCloskey*

Credits

Produced by: Sea-Hill Press, Inc.

6101 200th St. SW, Suite 205

Lynnwood, WA 98036

Telephone 425.697.3606

www.seahillpress.com

President: Greg Sharp

Editor: Wendy Slotboom

Technical Editor: Laura M. Reinstatler

Proofreader: Jamie Trubia

Photography: Ken Wagner

and Jay Dotson

Photo Styling: Sharon Yenter,

Jason Yenter, and Trish Carey

Art Direction and Design: Barbara Schmitt

Illustrations: Brian Metz

Blended Quilts from In The Beginning
© 2002 Sharon Evans Yenter
In The Beginning, Seattle, Washington USA

ISBN 0-9706900-1-0

Printed in Hong Kong

Bibliography

Allen, Gloria Seaman. *First Flowerings: Early Virginia Quilts*. Washington, D.C.: DAR Museum, 1987.

Amsden, Deirdre. *Colourwash Quilts*. Bothell, Washington: That Patchwork Place, 1994.

Bacon, Lenice Ingram. *American Patchwork Quilts*. New York, New York: William Morrow & Co. Inc., 1973. Reprinted: Bonanza Books, 1980.

Betterton, Shiela. *Quilts and Coverlets*. Bath, Great Britain: The American Museum in Britain, 1978.

Bullard, Lacy Folmar and Shiell, Betty Jo. *Chintz Quilts: Unfading Glory*. Tallahassee, Florida: Serendipity Publishers, 1983.

Colby, Averil. *Patchwork*. Newton Centre, Massachusetts: Charles T. Branford Co., 1958, 1978.

Dewhurst, C. Kurt and MacDowell, Betty and MacDowell, Marsha. *Artists in Aprons: Folk Art by American Women*. New York, New York: E.P. Dutton, 1979.

Holstein, Jonathan. *The Pieced Quilt, an American Design Tradition*. New York, New York: Little, Brown and Co., 1973.

Kiracofe, Roderick and Johnson, Mary Elizabeth. *The American Quilt: The History of Cloth and Comfort 1750-1950*. New York, New York: Clarkson N. Potter, Inc., 1993.

McCloskey, Marsha. *Block Party*. Emmaus, Pennsylvania: Rodale Press, 1998.

McCloskey, Marsha. *On to Square Two*. Bothell, Washington: That Patchwork Place, 1992.

Orlofsky, Myron and Patsy. *Quilts in America*. New York, New York: McGraw-Hill Book Co., 1974. Reprinted: Abbeville Press, 1992.

Pettit, Florence H. *America's Printed & Painted Fabrics*. New York, New York: Hastings House Publishers, 1970.

Quilters' Guild of Great Britain. *Quilt Treasures of Great Britain*. Nashville, Tennessee: Rutledge Hill Press, 1995.

Rae, Janet. *The Quilts of the British Isles*. New York, New York: E.P. Dutton, 1987.

Roy, Gerald E. *Blending the Old & the New*. Paducah, Kentucky: American Quilter's Society, 1997.

Vaessen, Dr. J.A.M.F., Director. *Quilts: The Dutch Tradition*. Arnhem, The Netherlands: Open-Air Museum, 1992.

Yenter, Sharon Evans. *Floral Bouquet Quilts*. Seattle, Washington: In The Beginning Publishing, 2001.

Yenter, Sharon Evans. *In The Beginning, Quilt Shop Series*. Bothell, Washington: That Patchwork Place, 1992.

Resources

Fabric collections by Sharon Yenter, and fabric collections and Precision Trimmers™ by Marsha McCloskey are available at your local quilt shop or you may inquire at:

> In The Beginning Fabrics
> 8201 Lake City Way NE
> Seattle, WA 98115
> 206.523.8862
> www.inthebeginningfabrics.com

Quilt Wall® is available at your local quilt shop or you may order from:

> Keepsake Quilting
> PO Box 1618
> Center Harbor, NH 03226-1618
> 1.800.865.9458